"Here is ministry on the w[...] assumptions are challenged and supplanted by the greatness of God's metanarrative."

Dr. John David Smith
Executive Director
BMA Missions

"This is an exciting story about one thinker's journey from agnosticism to faith. Anyone who has a heart to see the gospel advance will feel the thrill of seeing God at work in the human heart as you read this real-life account. This book will make most readers long to get into honest and humble discussions with their non-Christian friends."

Dennis McCallum
Author of *Walking In Victory*
Lead pastor of Xenos Christian Fellowship

"The Internet being what it is, there's more communicating than ever. It's less clear that there's much real conversation. Facebook being what it is, there's no lack of "friending." It's less clear that there's much real friendship. Real conversation and real friendship go together, and our world would be better if there were more of both. This book offers us a worthy model of what conversation and friendship can look like."

Preston Jones
Professor of History
John Brown University
Author (with Greg Graffin) of
Is Belief in God Good, Bad or Irrelevant?

"This is a great read for anyone who is serious about sharing their faith! I'm reminded of the process involved in sharing the gospel with a lost and wounded world. Thanks, Jack, for personalizing the power of the gospel and the work it takes to unpack the layers of just one life. I'm personally challenged and convicted to no longer look at people as projects but to take the time to embrace the 'messiness' of reaching those made in God's image."

Lee Epstein
Co-Directional Leader New Heights Church
Directional Leader Global Outfitters

"For every believer who longs to reach someone who seems unreachable . . . this is the book!"

Dr. Todd Ahrend
International Director
The Traveling Team

"From the classroom to the chat room, follow this fascinating and transforming conversation between Jack, a student, and Nick, a philosophy professor. Like riding a midnight roller coaster, you'll be amazed where it takes you. Hold on to your seat!"

Dr. Steve Shadrach
Director
Center for Mission Mobilization

TIPPING
OUR
KINGS

FINDING THE TRUTH
IN A WORLD FULL OF OPTIONS

JACK CRABTREE

BookVillages™

Tipping Our Kings: Finding the Truth in a World Full of Options
© 2012 by Jack Crabtree

All rights reserved. No part of this publication may be reproduced in any form without written permission from Book Villages, P.O. Box 64526, Colorado Springs, CO 80962. www.bookvillages.com.

BOOK VILLAGES and the BOOK VILLAGES logo are registered trademarks of Book Villages. Absence of ® in connection with marks of Book Villages or other parties does not indicate an absence of registration of those marks.

ISBN: 978-1-93851-210-0

Cover and interior design by Niddy Griddy Design, Inc.

Unless otherwise identified, all Scripture quotations in this publication are taken from The Holy Bible, English Standard Version Copyright © 2001 by Crossway Bibles, a division of Good News Publishers.

Holy Bible, New Living Translation, copyright © 1996, 2004, 2007 by Tyndale House Foundation. Used by permission of Tyndale House Publishers Inc., Carol Stream, Illinois 60188. All rights reserved.

All definitions in this publication are taken from Oxford English Dictionary, copyright © 2012 Oxford University Press. All rights reserved.

LCCN: 2012919056

Printed in the United States of America

16 15 14 13 12 / 1 2 3 4 5 6 7 8

Dedication

To Lael,
for making this conversation possible

Contents

Foreword
by George Walker

You cannot tell the wrong person the Gospel! There are still many who have yet to hear it and many more who need to *understand* it. The Good News of Christ dying for our sins and rising again is for every single human being on earth. Indeed, "everyone who calls on the name of the LORD will be saved." (Romans 10:13, NLT) God does not show favoritism. And no one is excluded.

This is where you and I come in. The scriptural remedy is clear, "But how can they call on him to save them unless they believe in him? And how can they believe in him if they have never heard about him? And how can they hear about him unless someone *tells* them?" (Romans 10:14, NLT, emphasis mine.)

The process is pretty simple isn't it?

Simple as it may be, if we are honest we must admit the fear of man remains our greatest challenge to obeying God's command to *tell* the Gospel. What a snare that can be! We often vacillate between fearing man and trusting God's enablement, don't we? The Bible readily acknowledges this reality, "Fearing people is a dangerous trap." (Proverbs 29:25, NLT) While our fear of *the very* people God desires to save is a definite hindrance, Scripture affirms that, "God has not given us a spirit of fear and timidity, but of power, love, and self-discipline. So never be ashamed to tell others about our Lord." (2 Timothy 1:7-8, NLT)

Oh, how we need His grace to walk boldly in this area of the Christian life! We need encouragement, and sometimes we just need someone to show us "how" to do it!

Let me assure you that in your hands you are holding a real-life, grassroots, practical example of *how* God helped a student overcome the fear barrier and changed the life of an intellectual forever. As Jack befriends Nick and begins to feel the weight of his "not-enoughness" the Lord enables him to deal with his fears, judge his own biases, and eventually welcome the hard questions of an inquiring soul. Nick's story demonstrates that the fear of telling the Gospel can be as real as the fear often associated with hearing the Gospel! Yet it also demonstrates there is hope for each of us—hope that the Lord can use *anyone*—even one in the midst of the fear and wrestling—to reach *anyone*.

If you, like Nick, are seeking God, looking for answers to your questions, or trying to find genuine meaning, it is no accident that you hold this book in your hands. There is a message here that offers a secure and steady anchor in a world swirling with failed relationships and limitless options—options that often produce stress, anxiety, loneliness, and depression.

Come with your questions. Come with your burdens. Come with your longings. You might be surprised to find that the answer to your search is the very *Person* who said, "Come to me, all of you who are weary and carry heavy burdens, and I will give you rest. Take my yoke upon you. Let me teach you, because I am humble and gentle at heart, and you will find rest for your souls." (Matthew 11:28-29, NLT) As He helped Jack overcome his fears to tell about Him, He can also help you overcome your fears to believe and follow Him!

George Walker
Co-founder
Worldview Resource Group
9-18-2012

A Brief Introduction

Not long after I began to take my faith seriously, I was thrown into the middle of a friendship with Nick—a brilliant, non-believing Ph.D. philosophy student who was also a walking thesaurus—not to mention a childhood chess-prodigy. Meeting Nick Chapman was more than cosmic coincidence, but at the time I had no clue our meeting held eternal significance.

From the coffee shop to the keyboard, from clarity to confusion and back again, my friendship with Nick was the most theologically stressful, stretching, surprising, thought-provoking time I've experienced. As George Walker, one of my favorite teachers, puts it, "I genuinely felt the weight of my own not-enough-ness." That's healthy!

That's how it's going to be with the people we encounter everyday. Talking to people is easy, but impacting lives is God's business, not ours. It must be Him working through us.

Will every question get tied up in a neat bow this side of the grave? No. Is that okay? It better be. If every question were answered, would we ever need to trust God? Life isn't about pretty bows; it's about getting to know the One who ties and unties them—the One who made the ribbon in the first place. It's about studying His knots with the instruction manual He's given us.

Sure. As we grow in our relationship with Him, we'll receive some answers. As we read what others before us have struggled through, our understanding will increase. The Christian life does not exist inside a vacuum.

If I'm not experiencing that weight of inadequacy, I'm stagnating—I'm not relying on the One with the answers. Feeling like you possess all the answers isn't healthy. Feeling like you hold enough answers is dangerous.

This book wrote itself because it was born out of my friendship and subsequent long-distance dialogue with Nick about God's nature and existence, mankind's purpose and current predicament, the prevalence of "needless" suffering in our world, and many other questions non-believers (and many believers) wrestle with today.

Intellectually, Nick and I are on different levels, but God's power is often shown through our weakness. God wanted to make sure He got all the credit, so He chose me to interact with Nick. I wouldn't trade that experience for anything!

No one is a lost cause. I wanted to write Nick off—I even judged him before I ever met him. What a huge mistake! I had to ask myself, "Do I value people regardless of their beliefs?" I came to understand that *everyone* has deep needs, but we often have to earn the right to hear them.

James' words also served me well, "Be quick to hear, slow to speak, slow to anger," (James 1:19). I had to be humble and genuinely interested in the other person. If I'm simply waiting for my turn to speak, I might as well walk out the door. I had to be willing to say, "I don't know, but I'll find out." Conversely, I couldn't allow my fear of looking foolish to paralyze my obedience to God's commission.

If I truly believe I serve a God who has all the answers, can I trust Him to provide them? I can, and they came—often in surprising ways.

In short, I put in the work, and God guided me. As Nick and I moved our pieces around the theological chessboard, an almighty Bobby Fischer was whispering in my ear.

Chapter One

Transitions and Tall Strangers

The University of Arkansas sits atop a hill in the northwest corner of the state in a pseudo-hippie town of 68,000 called Fayetteville. The city has been affectionately dubbed "Little Austin," by its laid-back inhabitants (many of whom sport stickers on their bumpers bearing the moniker—"Fayettechill").

A year had barely scraped by since I had graduated from the U.A. with a degree in journalism, and I was still in the area. As summer sprinted to a close, the temperature steadily encroached upon that dreaded triple-digit threshold, while the sweltering humidity practically forced me to swim to the mailbox.

Fayetteville's population plummets during the summer, when many of the 20,000 students leave town. I, too, was weeks away from joining the proverbial hajj, when I met one of those unique souls who deserved to be called an "individual"—Nicholas Chapman.

More precisely, my wife, Lael, met Nick and couldn't stop saying I needed to hang out with him before we moved to Wisconsin. "I ran into Jared at Arsaga's today and met his roommate, Nick." Lael had been a barista and Jared was one of her regulars. "Nick's getting his Ph.D. in philosophy and teaching a class at the U.A. It was kind of crazy, because we were just talking and suddenly Nick flat out asks me, 'So Lael, are you religious?' I was caught off-guard by his bluntness, and Jared just started laughing and gave me away. You know how Jared and I have had all those discussions about Christianity," Lael said, waiting for my nod of recollection before resuming her story.

"Once I told Nick I was a Christian, he just started grilling me about my faith. It was kind of neat, though, because he wasn't antagonistic about it at all. He just seemed genuinely interested in how I was going to respond."

My cynical side was getting the better of me, as Lael continued, "I really want you guys to meet, because I think you'll be able to give him a more solid response. You're just better at this kind of thing."

Stringing seemingly mismatched modifiers together, Lael carried on describing Nick. I'd never known anyone who fit the description, and the idea of meeting him made me feel uneasy—not to mention, a little threatened.

I had already constructed my philosophy-professor-stereotype and dismantling it seemed a daunting prospect. In a few short weeks, everything had to be packed and ready for our move to Wisconsin to attend Bible school, and I secretly hoped time would slip away and spare me the ordeal of slogging it out over religion with this guy. Could I handle all of his questions? Nick, simply put, was a distraction.

However, like any journalist worth his salt, I sought out a second source to corroborate Lael's testimony. A second opinion never hurts—especially when you're looking for an escape.

Sean "Iowa" Richards, who had been a friend of mine for most of my collegiate career, dropped by our apartment at Maple Manor. His hair was long. His smile was easy. Sean could have passed for a clean-mouthed iteration of Jeffrey Lebowski from that Coen brothers cult-classic. He was definitely into that whole brevity thing—he spoke in "abbrevs."

After catching Sean up on Lael meeting a philosophy guy, Sean scooted forward on the living room couch and said, "Oh, Nick Chapman? He was my prof. for Intro. to Philosophy. Nick's awesome, man," he laughed. "He called me Ziggy for some reason. That guy is too smart for his own good . . . and most of the class. I don't think many people got what he was saying half the time . . ." he trailed off, thinking. "I mean, his vocab. is ridic, and he doesn't know how to dumb it down, because it's just normal for him."

"Huh," was the only brilliant response my multitaskingly-challenged mind could conjure. "Is he a cool guy, though?" I asked. "I mean, is he that arrogant professor type?"

Sean laughed again and said, "No dude. Nick is super chill, but definitely socially awk. I mean, he looks like the epitome of . . . well, picture that stereotypical philosophy prof. in your head." He paused and let me imagine. "Whatever you're seeing—that's Nick."

My interest was piqued. "What was the first day of class like?"

An amused grin struck Sean's face. "So he walks in as the bell is ringing looking like he hasn't slept in three days, with dark circles under his eyes and about a week's worth of beard growth on his face and neck. Plus, he's wearing this old, baggy, striped bumblebee sweater, and glasses with those thick, plastic frames! It was awesome! I was like, 'Who is this guy? I mean, this is a philosophy prof!'"

"So, was he a decent professor, though?" I asked.

"Yeah, Nick's legit. I mean, he definitely knows his stuff. But about halfway through the semester I was kind of getting bored, because no one was interacting in class. So one day I decided, 'I'm just going to completely mess with Nick today.' And I just started raising my hand and asking tons of blatantly antagonistic questions!" He laughed. "Nick loved it! It was hilarious! I think he liked me after that."

That was different. "That's sort of refreshing that he was cool with you questioning him in the middle of class."

"Yeah, I think he enjoyed the change of pace. We started hanging out outside of class. You know Nick was like a childhood chess prodigy, right?" I nodded as Sean continued the story. "I played him once and held out for a few moves. Nick said I did better than most. I mean, he's kind of a professional, but I did beat his girlfriend!"

Sean had recently become a believer in college, so I asked him if he and Nick had ever talked about religion. "Yeah, that's pretty much all he asked me about," Sean began. "He was actually cool about it and a little surprised I had some answers."

As Sean closed our front door, guilt settled on me like a suffocating blanket. I knew I needed to meet Nick. Sure, lots of intelligent people are open-minded—just not usually about Christianity or the Bible. I had serious doubts that any of my words could change his mind and still planned to avoid an introduction.

A few days later, Lael and I met our friend, Grace, for a last coffee before our move north. A warm breeze was blowing, so we decided to sit at one of the small, round tables on the shop's front patio. After an hour of good conversation, our sand ran out, and as Grace walked away from our table, Nick and Jared materialized in front of us.

Now, you have to understand one thing about Nick and Jared. Not only were they roommates, but they were the only two bachelors in the entire philosophy doctorate program at the U.A.—they were married to their work. Additionally, they had both moved to Arkansas from out of state; hence, they weren't exactly social butterflies (by their own self-deprecating admission). In short, their social lives revolved mostly around each other and Jared's big black and white cat, Yoshi.

Whatever the reason, after some brief introductions, Nick asked what my favorite Monty Python film was, and we were soon deeply entrenched in conversation surrounding "Monty Python's Life of Brian," amongst other more philosophically-charged topics.

Much to my consternation, Nick revealed he had never seen the film and was surprised that I, as a Christian, liked it so much. (It was banned in several countries when it was originally released . . . I would argue mistakenly so). We made plans to arrange a proper introduction for him.

Thank you, Monty Python.

This was the beginning of several highly-caffeinated nights of frenzied conversation. Sadly, as summer shut down, Lael and I had less than a week before our trek to Wisconsin.

Why had I met Nick Chapman?

Chapter Two

Getting to Know You . . .

The next night, Lael and I drove to Nick and Jared's split-level apartment to watch the "Life of Brian." We started the movie, but Nick was more interested in peppering me with questions about theology. As I did my best to answer, I tossed a few personal questions back at Nick. Lael, in keeping with her late-night movie routine, had already fallen asleep on one of Nick's couches as one of the characters questioned from the TV, "Blessed are the cheese-makers?"

I asked Nick for his version of how he and Lael had met a few days earlier, and he recounted the story. "Yeah, last week Jared and I ran into Lael at Arsaga's, but Lael and Jared already knew each other. I asked her about the meaning of her name, because I like to ask those kinds of questions, I guess."

Lael told Nick her name meant "belonging to God," so Nick asked if she was a religious person. As soon as Jared heard this question, he rolled his eyes and sat down with his drink. "I rolled my eyes too, because I knew what I was in for—actually, I take that back. I knew that whatever happened was going to be combative, because Jared is a pretty committed atheist," Nick said.

As the unlikely trio discussed religion outside on the patio, an older man eavesdropped on their conversation from a nearby table. Lael recalled her experiences as a Christian, and Jared wasn't impressed. He wanted proof, not feelings. Nick laughed to himself as he told me the story and glanced around to make sure Jared was still downstairs. "Then Lael would be talking about some Bible passage, and that random old guy would interrupt her and try to tell her what the passage meant. She just owned him. He had nothing to say!"

Nick was surprised that Lael had known her Bible so well. I glanced over at Lael sleeping on the couch and felt no small measure of pride. My pride was short-lived, however, as Nick explained that most of the Christian students in his introductory philosophy classes were not reflective thinkers. "They don't even get combative when you talk about Nietzsche who said God is dead. They're just like, 'Oh. That guy was wrong.' You know?"

As Nick said these words, I couldn't help feeling somewhat responsible. I hadn't always been willing to put tough questions to my faith. Questions hadn't always been encouraged, either.

"So I kind of admired Lael's wieldy intellect," Nick began, "and she also asked Jared a really good question: 'Why are you an atheist?'" Jared had deflected the question by insisting that the burden of proof lay solely on Lael. He didn't think he needed to prove that God didn't exist.

Nick quickly came to Lael's aid, though, and said, "Jared, you know, logically that doesn't hold up. You're making an epistemic[1] claim. You're saying, 'I know that God does not exist.' In order to make that claim, you have to support that position. Otherwise, don't make the claim. Say, 'I don't know.' Or say you're an ignostic."

I had never heard the term ignostic, so Nick explained. "An ignostic is different from an agnostic. An ignostic would not only say they don't know enough to know there is a God, they would say it's impossible to ever know enough. But Jared had to say, 'No. I'm not an ignostic. I'm an atheist. I do not believe in God.'"

Both Nick and Lael continued to press Jared for justification

---

1. Epistemic: of or relating to knowledge or to the degree of its validation.

regarding his atheistic beliefs, but he couldn't provide any and began to get flustered. Nick confessed from the adjacent couch, "You know, I did feel bad for Jared, but that's the typical atheistic position to take: 'I'm not the one who needs to prove anything. You're the one who needs to provide proof.' But it's a really bad argument."

Before the discussion got out of hand, two of Jared's students arrived at the coffee shop, and the topic was dropped. Nick was intrigued by Lael though. "I was thinking that I'd kind of like to see her again in the context of Jared. I'd like to see my roommate get reamed by this little 4' 11" girl. I think the next time I saw her was with you."

The effects of my journalism degree had yet to wear off, and I sometimes got stuck in interview mode. Actually, I majored in journalism because I enjoy hearing (and telling) people's stories. Since I knew next to nothing of Nick's history, I thought I'd better begin at the beginning. "So where were you born?"

"Norwalk, Connecticut," he replied. His answer surprised me, because his voice had never betrayed a trace of a New England accent. "Yeah, we lived pretty close to Yale—close to New Haven—because my dad commuted to New York each day. I guess my parents wanted to stay close to the border. So I'm not fully a product of Tennessee—we moved there when I was twelve," he said in his semi-slur fashion. "That probably explains why I don't have a southern accent either." Nick paused to think. "Well, that, and my mom is German and my dad was from the Bronx."

"Sounds like a real linguistic melting-pot," I said as Nick took a drink of his tea and raised his eyebrows in confirmation. My mind went back to the chess career he had alluded to on the night we met, and I asked about who had influenced him the most.

"Oh man," he mumbled to himself before coming to a decision.

"Alright, I'm gonna go with Bobby Fischer on this one, and I'm choosing him for his fortitude, his temerity, his kind of unabashed individualism, and his level of commitment to a discipline that was unpopular at the time. People didn't really care about chess, but he had a relentless devotion to the art of chess. He had an ethic, a code about chess playing, that had a certain sacrosanct[2] value to it—even though it didn't carry over into his personal life. Those are the things I cherish about his life. If you can be that impassioned about something, it really says something about your character—about your ethos."

"So you're picking him from a purely 'chess-playing' standpoint?" I clarified.

"Exactly," he said quickly. "A purist—almost idealist notion."

"Gotcha. So if you could be transported anywhere, at any time to ask anyone one question, who would you ask and what would you ask them?" I know it sounds silly, but this question can be pretty revealing—especially if someone has an unresolved question in his or her life. Since Nick was getting a Ph.D. in philosophy, I expected him to have plenty of questions for guys like Plato and Barth.

"It'd have to be—yeah, it'd have to be Gutenberg. I would ask something like, 'Did you really have to invent the printing press?'" he paused, straight-faced, then laughed, "No, I'm just kidding. But it was only the greatest invention ever, you know?" Nick's dry sarcasm rose to Death Valley levels as he said, "Most people would be like, 'Well, I'd go back and ask Jesus if He was really God?' Not me. I'm talking to Gutenberg!"

"Well, in keeping with the printing press motif, what's your favorite word at the moment?"

---

2. Sacrosanct: (especially of a principle, place, or routine) regarded as too important or valuable to be interfered with.

Without hesitation, he said, "Probably 'lugubrious.'"

"Define that." I had no clue what it meant.

"Lugubrious means being in a mournful state to an exaggerated end."

"Why is that your favorite word?" I asked, fearing my questions had made him suicidal.

Nick shrugged. "It just popped into my head."

"Lugubrious. . . ." I mumbled. As, "Always look on the bright side of life . . ." emanated from the TV, I glanced up and saw the credits rolling. This had been pre-game banter, and I was excited to talk to Nick again. Maybe we'd eventually play some real theological chess.

Chapter Three

Not Quite a Master

A few days later, I took a break from feverishly packing up our apartment and decided to meet Nick at Arsaga's again. Hanging out with him was turning into a form of stress-relief, because he always seemed so calm and our conversation was easy. When I rolled into the parking lot, I spotted his car instantly. The rusted white Honda Accord with the matte black hood had as much character as its owner. Nick told me he drove that car because he'd wrecked his previous one. He'd actually wrecked several.

The old film "Searching for Bobby Fischer" comprised the extent of my knowledge of competitive chess, so I was eager to hear about life as a chess prodigy. I wondered if he still played and what made him want to get a Ph.D. in philosophy. We ordered our drinks, and while the barista pulled shots for my Americano, I asked Nick about his first chess game ever.

"I was five, when I played my grandfather. He's one of the most competitive people I know," Nick began. "He played out a couple of moves, and then he check-mated me. He just laughed, and when I looked up at him, all he said was, 'You didn't develop your pieces right.'"

"You were five?" I was astonished at how competitive a grandfather could be with a five-year-old. I worried about possible psychological damage.

"My grandfather did the same thing to my mom, when she was young, and she hasn't played since."

"Did you ever play him again?" I asked.

"I did, but not for a while. One day I was on my computer, saw the chess program, and started messing around with it. Something sort of clicked, and it was like I understood how the pieces were moving, and that in an attack against someone you want to compile your pieces to that side of the board. After I started beating the computer, I began playing my dad and wiping the floor with him."

We grabbed our drinks and made for a booth in the corner. I couldn't get over how casually Nick talked about beating the computer. He never sounds like he's bragging, because these things seem normal for him.

As we slid into the booth, Nick's intensity grew, like a Bond villain recounting his master plan. "I was studying the pattern recognition, the piece placement, and everything that goes into the strategy of a chess game, and I was doing it in a way that I thought would give me a chance against my grandfather. I would go over games by Fischer and try to figure out why he would move in certain ways. The next time I played my grandfather, I won. He resigned by tipping his king over and said, 'I have no use for playing you anymore.' I was thirteen."

Nick's level of determination and competitiveness surprised me, because he always struck me as incredibly relaxed. Most competitive people have trouble debating without becoming emotionally driven. Emotion can cloud logic, but Nick always seemed to remain calm even when he disagreed with something.

After beating his grandfather, Nick began playing chess at a competitive level but decided that if he didn't earn his grandmaster title by his early twenties, he'd give it up. This normally requires 2,500 rating points—Nick leveraged all his energy toward his chess career.

"I got to about 2,172, when I was 15. That made me one of the top-ranked players under 21 in the country. I only needed to win a few more games to reach the master level."

In chess there's a phenomenon called blindfold chess, where two players sit across from each other and play an entire game in their heads with no board or pieces. They simply picture everything in their minds and call out the coordinates for each move. I couldn't comprehend what Nick told me next. On more than one occasion he has played and won ten blindfold games—simultaneously.

"I don't need to look at the boards—I memorize them," he said. "That's where my true talent in chess lies. It's just you and your opponent, but your moves speak for you. Playing chess enthralled me. It's a rush that lasts a long time."

"Did you ever get to play a grandmaster?" I asked.

Nick played Julian Hodgson, a grandmaster rated close to 2,550, and he was the toughest opponent Nick ever faced. "Kasparov, one of the greatest players ever, was rated around 2,730. When I played Julian Hodgson, I had never been paired with a grandmaster in tournament chess."

Nick said he made the grandmaster nervous. "I took a lot of time off his clock, but he got away with a win. Afterward he brought me to the grandmaster room, where there were these big pints of beer and whatnot. I was only sixteen, but I thought, 'Well, I'll go ahead and partake.' We analyzed our chess game for about an hour and a half, while drinking brewskies and meeting what I call 'chess celebrities'—including the beautiful Polgar sisters. I'd say that was one of the funniest and most unexpected moments I can remember from playing tournament chess," he said looking out the window.

I asked how he balanced high school with competitive chess, and he said, "I would often play chess until really late and then try and get up early enough to get my homework done. The first year, I cut back on chess tournaments, because I was struggling academically." I couldn't imagine Nick struggling with academics—something that now consumed his life. What had flipped that academic switch?

"By my sophomore year, I knew I would never be a grandmaster—much less a great grandmaster like Bobby Fischer. For the first time, I felt depression with a certain gravity to it, because most of my identity was built into that chess stereotype," he confessed.

Nick took a sip of his Italian soda, still nearly full, and I glanced down at my empty mug. Nick told me he still took mood-stabilizers, and I wondered if giving up the chess dream had kick-started his downward spiral.

I felt a kinship with Nick. During a few years of teenage angst, my mother worried about me. Finally she asked whether I thought I needed to be on anti-depressants, but, full of pride, I had shunned the idea of taking pills as a sign of weakness. Looking back, I wonder if I could have made those last high school years much easier on myself. "So you had your first real problems with manic-depression during your sophomore year?" I asked.

"Mood disturbances?" he restated. "Yeah, midway through my sophomore year, a teacher I trusted came up to me and said, 'You've been kind of down lately. You know, I know someone in town who might be able to take care of this.' He referred me to the most intellectual psychologist in town—Bruce." Nick's first session with Bruce went something like this:

Bruce: Why are you here, Nicholas?
Nick: Oh, well, I'm depressed.
Bruce: Why do you think you're depressed?
Nick: Well, if happiness is supposed to be the end goal of life, and you feel that happiness is unattainable, then in some sense you're not able to finish your life's task. That's depressing.

Bruce: That's true.

As I thought about Nick's statement, I began to see how empty his life must have seemed. He was searching for significance in something greater than himself, while his identity in the chess community was crumbling around him. As I sat on the other side of the booth, I could see that his search appeared to be ongoing.

Nick's manic-depression wasn't caused solely by chess, though. "There were other factors. With chess, there was a distinct moment when I felt depressed, but chess was definitely not the onset of a larger mood disturbance. Most of my high school depression had to do with the strained relationship I had with my dad."

Nick summed up home-life as tumultuous. "As my dad's oldest child, he wasn't used to raising a kid. He didn't know how to raise a kid, and his exacting punishments altered or modified my character in some ways," he said regretfully.

Nick's parents had extremely high expectations for him. He's the oldest of four siblings, and they all acknowledge that he had it the worst. In a puzzled tone Nick continued, "I don't even know how I let them down. But even in chess, for instance, if I wasn't coming home with first prize, my dad wasn't interested in me."

After Nick won the Tennessee state chess tournament, his dad "gave credence to it," but Nick didn't think he really cared. "I developed a pretty hard heart when it came to my dad, because he wasn't there for me. He wasn't a 'father.' An 'absentee dad' maybe. To this day, I care about him, but I'm just not sure if I could say that I love my dad," Nick said, appearing to wish things were different.

"What do you think brought out most of the conflict with your dad?" I asked.

"I was lazy and didn't react well to menial work. So in the summers after I was sixteen, my dad wanted me to get a job—which was a normal expectation," he said. Nick recalled that he had been fired more than once for bagging groceries incorrectly—the bread and eggs apparently did not belong on the bottom. "It was obvious that I wasn't making it in the work world."

Nick's dad released his frustration verbally. "There were times when the things he would yell at me just seemed out of spite. I mean, there was nothing didactic[1] about it. He'd blow up to the point of no return and say some really, really mean things—maybe to get a reaction out of me? I don't really know. But if I reacted to him, he would get angrier. So yeah, chess wasn't at the top of the list, you know?"

Suddenly, my teenage depression seemed pitifully weak. "Did you guys ever set things right?" I asked.

"He's talked to me about how bad he felt that he wasn't more proactive when I was feeling depressed, for instance. I never heard anything from my dad when I was seeing psychiatrists and psychologists, though. He was just backing away from it all because he just didn't know what to say or do."

Nick's demeanor softened slightly as he continued, "After his heart transplant, which was about five years ago, I noticed that his attitude and personality just changed. And ever since then, he's been a very good dad for the most part."

Nick was wounded and still a long way from recovery. I felt guilty for the stable home-life I'd experienced. My parents had always been there for me, and supported my dreams—even the foolish ones. They also modeled Christianity for me, and even apologized when the model broke down. I knew Nick wasn't a Christian, but I wondered whether he'd been exposed to the church or religion in any way. Had his experience with his father affected his view of God?

Nick related his upbringing in the Episcopalian church. His

---

1. Didactic: intended to teach, particularly in having moral instruction as an ulterior motive.

family stopped attending when they moved to Tennessee, and nothing from those first twelve years in church stuck out in his memory, except the communion wine.

Nick was exposed to a shallow version of Christianity. "I never had an informed grasp of what Christianity actually means or understood the contextually sensitive features of it, the narrative, the historical setting, the ramifications for certain modes of living. Those are the biggest questions a human being can ask. I think they're bigger questions than even philosophy can ask. And those questions were never dealt with," he remarked with flat-lined enthusiasm, before likening church membership to joining a country club.

A sinking nausea grew in the pit of my stomach. Nick's church frustrated me for not giving him a better grasp of the deep truths found in God's Word. At least he believed Christianity should deal with important issues. His experience with the church hadn't filled the void he felt in his life, and his lack of emotion left me with nothing more to say. I changed the subject and asked how his parents met.

"My parents told me they met on a train, but then my grandparents told me the truth—they met through a dating service, and my dad showed up smoking cigarettes. He just wanted to go get a steak with this girl he'd met. She was twenty-one. He was thirty-five." Nick said he sometimes tells people the train version, because it sounds better.

"What's your favorite memory of your dad from when you were young?" I asked.

Without a moment's hesitation Nick said, "When I was in middle school, he did something that captured my heart. This group of kids stole my shoes on the bus, and they were walking down to their houses—one of them wearing my shoes. So I walked through the front door crying, and my dad was like, 'What's wrong, Nick? What's wrong?' I mumbled, 'They stole my shoes,' and my dad got into an incredible rage, walked out there, and said, 'Who has my son's shoes?' Literally, three minutes later, he walked through the front door with my shoes and said, 'Don't worry. They're not going to steal your shoes anymore.' It was the first time my dad stuck up for me, and it means a lot to me even today," he said.

That memory seemed to act as a counterbalance for all the hard times. "So tell me one of the best memories of your mom from when you were younger," I said.

"Playing 'hooky' and going to eat at the mall. We did that a lot," he said. "We did that a lot more than we told my dad! Sometimes my mom would come to school at ten in the morning and say, 'I need to take Nick out for a little while. Grandpa's having problems,' or whatever. And we'd just go to the mall, hang out, and eat, and it was a wonderful day."

Nick's relationships with his mom and dad were drastically different. Nick said his mom was the only woman he ever loved, because no matter how badly he screwed up, she was always there for him. "My mom was amazing. One reason I decided not to kill myself was that I couldn't stand the thought of leaving this world apart from her. Out of all the family members I have, I would miss my mom the most. Sometimes she says, 'I love you.' It's rare, but she does say it," he said reverentially before continuing.

"My dad wanted to toss me out into the world to see what I could make of this life." he said. "He's praised me on a couple of levels. One: he's very proud I never killed myself. And two: he's proud of my education. Unfortunately, it was usually just me alone with some really messed up emotional issues, and he hadn't been there to help me."

While downcast and introspective, Nick still betrayed no anger in his voice or demeanor—just a puzzled stillness. As he looked out the window, his humanity hit me in the face. Nick was no longer an invincible professor with all the answers—he was human and needed a father's approval.

Chapter Four

Ambien + Adderall = Normal?

Even though Lael and I were moving the next day, she let me hang out with Nick one last time. I knew our meeting wasn't accidental, and I wanted to make the most of the little time we had left. I met Nick at his apartment and sat down across from him on the couch.

As I looked around his living room, a stack of books on Plato towered precariously next to his laptop on a large desk in the corner. When I indicated the stack, he explained that the overdue pile was related to his dissertation. "There's a barren shelf in the library thanks to me! I feel bad for undergrads who want to write on Plato because they won't be getting those back for a while," he said with mock concern.

I laughed and wondered when Nick had turned into an intellectual. "So where did you go to school when you were younger, and what was it like?" I asked.

Nick's face fell as he began to describe his middle school experience. "The Knoxville middle school was very violent and racist. They say, 'If you can't do, teach. If you can't teach, teach gym. And if you can't teach gym, you end up at my middle school.'" he said with a completely straight face. "I quickly made myself known as kind of a smart guy, but at my middle school, you couldn't be distinguished academically without adverse social repercussions. Kids would usually come in groups and beat me up just for being a skinny, little, white kid. I was scared a lot of the time," he said.

After Nick got a perfect score on one of the standardized tests, one of his teachers didn't think the school's environment was right for him and told his parents as much. She suggested Nick attend Webb School of Knoxville, a prestigious private school in the area—a place that would nurture Nick's intellect rather than stuff it in a locker.

"What was Webb like? Was it any better?" I asked.

"Yeah, violence was de-emphasized, and if you actually got into a fight with someone, you were immediately expelled. It was a completely different atmosphere," he said. "One of the first things I noticed was the dress code. It was suit and tie—we had to wear slacks, Oxford shirts, ties, blazers, the right shoes, the right socks, but all the cool kids were academically distinguished. The competition was cutthroat, and a lot of them were shooting for Ivy League schools. People said they studied six hours a day outside of class."

"How'd you get in?"

"I had to take this brutal six-hour preliminary exam, but I really wanted to go there."

"Wow. How do you think Webb helped you the most?" I asked.

"I'd say it cultivated my intellect writ large and taught me two things: how to write a critical paper, and how to really study. And those two gifts let me coast throughout the rest of high school and into all the schools I went to afterward. For the first year and a half I struggled," he admitted. "I can't think of any other time, even up through working on my doctorate, where I struggled as much with the routine of academic life."

His answer resonated with me. I'd had a particular journalism professor who was extremely tough. She threw you in over your head, and then worked with you until you got it right. Her class was the hardest I ever took, but it prepared me for the future. "Is there any one person you would credit with helping you make that transformation?" I asked.

Nick recounted the two high school teachers at Webb who influenced him the most. "My sophomore English teacher gave me a zero the first time I handed in a paper and said I could rewrite it. He didn't care whether I comprehended what happened in a book. He said I needed to say something about that comprehension. So that was a big difference from giving a book report, like you do in middle school. He wanted critical papers where you're coming up with a thesis and arguing it."

Nick continued, "And I also had a teacher, who I now call 'my theologian friend' or 'Doc,' who got me into philosophy and subjects like that—which is funny, because he just texted me," Nick said as he glanced down at his phone. "I looked up to those two teachers the most, and I think by my junior year, ironically, I had begun to write like a philosopher. I was writing philosophical essays, and one of my English teachers picked up on it."

"Was that when you began to think you'd want to focus on philosophy?" I asked

"When my English teacher said I wrote philosophically, I didn't really know what he meant. I didn't even have a great vocabulary. But by my freshman year in college, I decided I would specialize in philosophy. I remember reading a book on Wittgenstein called *The Duty of Genius* by Ray Monk, and I read some Nietzsche," he recalled. "Those were the only two I went through carefully. And if you read Nietzsche when you're lonely, it sounds like he's writing to you," he quipped.

Nick said that whenever the subject of finding the right university would come up, he became extremely passive. "We had college fairs, and I didn't want to partake in them, so my mom mentioned this school one day where all they do is read books. It's called the Great Books Program through St. John's College in New Mexico. When they took a look at the price tag, they were like,

'Oh gosh, that's a lot of money!' That's when I became interested, you know? If my parents didn't like it, I was like, 'Whoa! Maybe this is good!'"

Nick's mom filled out the application, and Nick was accepted about a week later. "They were really prompt, and called me to invite me out with the other prospective students. That was the extent of my college application experience," he said.

"Were you worried about being so far from home?" I asked.

"Well, that was about the time I was having problems with my moods and stuff, and the psychiatrist hadn't quite stabilized me to the point where I was thinking rationally about what I wanted to do. St. John's was a bad mix," he declared. "I was coming off of a summer where my dad and I were just at each other's throats, and I couldn't wait to get out of there. But as soon as I arrived in New Mexico, I felt homesick," he confessed. "It was strange and new but also very remote and isolated. I didn't want to go back to my dad or anything like that, but I felt pretty lonely too. Then I met a girl named Aleta, and we started dating, but I also started getting into drugs and acting out in ways I shouldn't have been. I really needed to leave."

"So did you recognize you were becoming unstable, or did someone have to point it out to you?" I asked.

"Aleta's sister indirectly pointed it out to me, when she visited her. She was so worried about me that she mentioned it to her parents, and guess who her parents called?" he asked. "Of all the people in the world to call, they called the dean, and I was called into his office. Aleta said, 'Don't worry about it. All he's going to do is give you a slap on the wrist, and we'll get on with things.' But I walked in there, and the dean said, 'Well, Mr. Chapman, either I can expel you, or you can take a forced medical leave.'"

Nick couldn't believe it, and then out of the corner of his eye, he saw the social worker he had seen two or three times while attending St. John's. "She promised me confidentiality and then repeated stuff verbatim to the dean that I had said to her, which really angered me. She had basically lied to me." Nick mimicked the social worker's concerned voice, "Well, you're a threat to yourself and to the school."

Even though Aleta was upset with the situation, Nick knew the social worker was right. "It was a blessing because things would've just gotten worse. I needed to go home because I was taking literally any drug that was offered to me, ya know? Just for the experience."

"So what happened next?" I asked.

"Well, I wanted to go back to St. John's—mainly because of Aleta and a couple of friends. You know, what do you do when you fall off your horse? You get back on. Things were going okay, but I still wasn't into the curriculum. I was there for the wrong reasons, but I did finish a full year," he said. "When August came, Aleta and I had broken up in kind of a bitter way, and the place was incestuous. I mean, I saw the same people over and over, and seeing her was weird."

Nick called his parents, and his dad picked up on his loneliness. "My dad never talks on the phone. He hates the phone, but he picked up and said, 'How's it going, Ace?' When my dad really likes me, he calls me Ace. So I explained things, and he said coming home would probably be good for me."

Nick took the entire semester off and came to terms with his medications and getting emotionally stable. His dad didn't bother him at all. "I think he was acknowledging that he couldn't force it out of me. I can't think of one constructive thing I did that semester, but it was nice getting stabilized. So that was St. John's."

"But you still needed to finish your undergrad, right?"

"Yeah, it's funny. I ended up at three more schools. I went to another school my mom discovered in Washington State called Evergreen State College. My experience there was interesting, because I was housed with drug dealers," he remarked off-handedly.

"Professional drug dealers?"

"They were just kids, but each one had a different drug they liked—which they sold for profit. They even showed me how to cut certain drugs. So I came in there with an Associate's in pharmacology and left with a Master's. I wasn't learning anything in class, though, and after my second independent study in philosophy, the teacher said I should go to Reed College in Portland, Oregon to get a degree in philosophy. I thought that was kind of weird, but I was looking to get out anyway. So I talked it over with my parents, and they were like, 'Gosh, it's expensive.' And it was really expensive. At the time, Reed College was considered the Harvard of the West, and sort of on the same track as Berkeley—it had that kind of weird prestige."

Despite a high level of academic excellence, Nick said the students at Reed were generally unhappy. "There was a girl I knew, and during break one day she killed herself. And I don't want to repeat myself, but people were very unhappy there. They weren't jovial. They wouldn't smile or say, 'Hi,' when you walked by—I just found it very strange."

"Was there an upside?" I asked.

"Being in class was the only thing that fit for me. The students were smart, so for the first time I felt like I belonged academically in a community," he said.

"So the philosophy program was good?"

"It was excellent," came the immediate response. "I should have finished up there, because I would have gotten into a much better grad school. They really only did contemporary analytic philosophy, which is precisely the kind of philosophy I shy away from. Just to give you a rundown, that branch of philosophy focuses on or emphasizes logic and linguistic analysis to solve philosophical problems or puzzles. And I'm more into the history of ideas—more literary philosophy—than working out symbols and proofs. So it wasn't quite the bent I was looking for, but the kids were tracking—they were smart."

"What was your favorite thing about Reed?" I questioned.

"All of my professors were really well qualified to teach and were engaging and entertaining. That's something I just didn't see at other schools," he said.

"What was your social life like at that time?" I asked.

"Well, my mom requested that I not have a roommate at Reed, because of my insomnia. I was up at weird hours—kind of like now. At Reed I became known as 'Dr. Nick,' because people would come up and ask me drug-related questions—stupid questions like, 'Should I smoke this Vicodin?' And I'm like, 'No, you don't wanna smoke Vicodin. Trust me. It's not going to get you lifted!'" he said before continuing.

"The mantra or motto for Reed is that they work hard and party hard, but to me they worked hard and partied stupidly. I'd give them advice, but they wouldn't invite me to the parties!" he said in a confounded tone. "Dr. Nick stuck because of an incident when I took a bunch of Ambien and walked across campus challenging people to chess. I was winning, but people just thought I was drunk, because when you get really toppled on Ambien, you function like a drunk person would. People were like, 'Wow, this guy's pretty interesting. He gets drunk and still wins chess games.'"

Later that semester Nick got a prescription for Adderall, because his doctor wanted to balance the Ambien out a little. Nick didn't have any more exploits. I asked if his thoughts about religion had changed since his early days in the church.

"No. Nothing changed," came Nick's quick response. "Most of the 'Reedies' I met were atheistic, and I wasn't getting any reinforcement from the Christian community—nor seeking it. So, yeah. You could say I was pretty spiritually impoverished, you know?" he said.

"So were you agnostic or atheistic or—"

"I'd probably say 'ignostic,' just in the sense that I didn't really think I had an ability to know, let alone define the God everyone was talking about. Some say 'agnostic' which is basically saying, 'I'm not sure.' But they don't rule out the possibility that they could be sure. I didn't even think I had the strength to know."

"So the question was just completely irrelevant to you?"

"Yeah, exactly. I was never an atheist."

"Why?"

"I don't know what it was, but I think I saw a certain 'contrarianism' in most of them—almost like a reactionary would have. I find atheists just so boring. I can't think of anything more watered-down and predictable than atheistic humanism. So I always kept hope alive that I might develop some middle position that might be interesting."

After a year at Reed, Nick attended the University of Tennessee and finished his undergraduate degree in ease. He took several basic courses, while enrolled in three graduate level philosophy classes. "I won the essay contest for the philosophy department and then had to go to a freshman class—Econ 101."

"So how did you end up at Arkansas?"

"After I finished my undergraduate degree, I went to Los Angeles and earned a Masters degree in philosophy from Loyola Marymount University. Then I began Duquesne's doctoral philosophy program, but had to leave because the program had funding issues. After scrambling for doctoral programs with rolling admissions, I found the University of Arkansas."

"Well, I'm glad you did!" I said, "It's crazy when you look at all the situations that had to work out perfectly for us to even meet. We'll definitely have to hang out whenever we're back in town on breaks from Wisconsin. So what are you working on this semester?"

"Well, I'm teaching an intro philosophy class, and I'll hopefully defend my dissertation prospectus at some point," he said.

"What's that?"

"The prospectus is like a pitch meeting for the idea behind your entire dissertation. I'll have to convince them that my dissertation is worth doing. Hopefully I'll defend before the semester is over, so I can begin working on the actual dissertation."

"Do you know what your prospectus will be about?" I asked.

"I have some ideas, but I'm not completely set. I'll let you know more when I'm sure about it. It will concern Plato in some way though," he said with glance at the stack of books on the desk.

Nick and I talked a little more before I had to leave. We were quickly becoming friends—and I enjoyed talking with him. I think he enjoyed being able to unload some of his baggage on someone, and I wanted more than anything to help him in any way I could. A sudden pang of sadness hit me as I realized this was most likely going to be the last night I'd see Nick face-to-face for quite some time. Sadness? Just days earlier I had viewed him as a mere distraction. Surely there was a bigger reason for our friendship.

Chapter Five

Speaking of Worldviews . . .

Shortly after meeting Nick, Lael and I found ourselves moving boxes into a "cozy" studio-apartment on the New Tribes Bible Institute (NTBI) campus in Waukesha, Wisconsin. As I carried the first box across the threshold, all the wonderful stories of pleasant Wisconsin summers—with their Edenic conditions—incinerated before my eyes. We had no AC and just happened to arrive during an unusually warm (hellish) summer.

The weather, however malevolent it seemed, could not diminish our excitement. Two years of biblical classes represented the next baby step toward our goal: planting an indigenous church among an unreached tribal group.

Lael and I soon found ourselves in a class called Evangelism in a Postmodern World—a course which took a bird's-eye-view of the evolution of predominant worldviews and thought-systems throughout history, with a sprinkling of Christian apologetics, and contextual evangelistic practices thrown in for good measure.

A worldview can be described as a metanarrative—an overarching story in which diverse themes and smaller stories find their appropriate place. Everyone constructs their own big picture story (whether they are aware of it or not) that forms the lens through which they view life, make sense of reality, and find their proper place in it. Everyone has a worldview, though many of the explanations their worldview offers are simply accepted and seldom examined.

To aid his students in gaining a more tangible grasp on just how different and inconsistent most everyone's personal worldview can be, our teacher handed us "worldview surveys" and instructed us to solicit complete strangers for their answers to some of the most fundamental questions about, well, fundamentals, I guess.

I cheated.

I found myself, however, in a pinch for the second survey. Lael and I returned to Waukesha late Monday night after a long Labor Day weekend (a time not conducive to homework of any kind). As I walked through the door toward the refrigerator, something caught my eye. On the kitchen counter lay my blank worldview survey—due in the morning. I needed a savior!

Enter the perfect guy for the job: Nick Chapman. Since Nick had already told me about his troubles with insomnia, I felt fairly confident I would not disturb his sleep and hoped he would enjoy the thought-provoking questions.

"Besides," I reasoned with myself, "I'm sure Nick has already thought through these questions." Extremely curious to hear his answers, I got Nick on the horn and after some preliminary pleasantries, launched into the survey.

Here are the sixteen questions I asked Nick:

1. How did human beings originate?
2. Is there any reason for human existence? Explain.
3. What happens to a person after they die?
4. What features, if any, distinguish humans from animals?
5. At birth, human beings are: selfish, innocent, a blank slate, or other?
6. Name two things you consider to be evil.
7. How did you decide that these were in fact evil?
8. How did evil come into existence?
9. What gives human beings the ability to reason or think logically?

10. Where do morals, values, ethics, and standards come from?
11. Is there any truth that is absolute? If yes, give two examples.
12. Is there anything real besides what our five senses show us? If so, how can you know it is in fact real?
13. Which of the following best describes your view of God:
    1) Creator of the universe but no longer involved
    2) Creator of the universe and still involved in the affairs of humans
    3) Not the creator but the essence of all that exists
    4) If none of the above, give a brief explanation
14. What shaped your belief or understanding about these things?
15. What would be the chief purpose of man (individually & communally)?
16. If you were wrong in your views, would you want to know?

Nick is on speakerphone, and Lael is walking through the kitchen where I'm sitting—which isn't unusual, since our living room, bedroom and kitchen are in all actuality the same room. Here's what Nick said:

Nick: Do you guys deal much with apologetics[1]? Or is that just something you kind of sidestep?

Jack: Oh no, we're actually in an apologetics class right now.

Lael: Nick, we know you hate apologetics. Don't hide it . . .

Nick: You're right, Lael. You're completely right. I don't like people imposing a priori[2] dictates on God's nature as opposed to the

---

1. Apologetics: reasoned arguments or writings in justification of something, typically a theory or religious doctrine.
2. *a priori*: relating to or denoting reasoning or knowledge that proceeds from theoretical deduction rather than from observation or experience, namely knowledge that can be known independent of experience.

way God dialectically reveals Himself to you on a personal level. I'm trying to assimilate that, though I'm not doing a very good job.

Jack: Well, for that worldview class, our assignments include surveys, where we ask people questions about their personal worldview. I just wanted to ask you those questions.

Lael: Because we knew you'd give good answers, Nick!

Jack: We also figured it would impress our instructors here.

Nick: Well, I think your teachers would say something like, "We should dismiss this on a priori grounds." You know what I mean? I don't sleep . . . I'm delusional . . . usually I can formulate myself better via e-mail. But if you want me to give answers right now, I'll do that too. Doesn't matter to me.

Jack: There are only sixteen questions, and you can be as brief or long-winded as you like.

Nick: Okay. Let me reflect on it. [no pause] Okay, yeah, I'm ready.

Jack: Let's do it.

1. How did human beings originate?

Nick: Wow. I was hoping for something like, "What is your favorite color?" Okay, well, I would say there was something like an Aristotelian prime mover—a prime mover in the sense of something, which obviously cannot be affected, but something which affects. And I think its manifestations (or its effects) produced or engendered images that were in its likeness. That would be the origination of human beings. So it's almost like a conception of god that is not quite the "Christian God." But the emanation or beings that you find from this first cause would be the rationale behind the original existence of humans. That is my first answer. Did I get it right?

Jack: Oh, I think . . . definitely.

2. Is there any reason for human existence? Explain.

Nick: Absolutely. Victory, triumph, and happiness, for one thing. Meaning, purpose, and existence are based in something that is existential, which essentially means we create our own meaning. At least that's what the generic solution indicates, but I have a different view. I believe that purpose and meaning are not something humans can simply create, but that they are based in a personal project that involves the inter-subjective, and in some cases, will involve your personal relationship to God.

Did that answer your question? Basically, I'm saying that there has to be the personal, the social, and the divine as the three constituents of making life meaningful or purposeful.

3. What happens to a person after they die?

Nick: That's a good question. Okay. So I think there's a real problem with Aquinas, who believed that the soul of a human, after it died, subsisted or remained in existence on some minimal level. And if a soul subsists, it can't be individuated, because it doesn't have any matter that it's embodied by.

So essentially I think that after death we have souls that are kind of going about in the ether without any individuation. And once the Resurrection occurs, that's when our souls will be infused with some type of individuating element.

4. What features, if any, distinguish humans from animals?
Nick: Rationality and laughter.

5. At birth, human beings are: selfish, innocent, a blank slate, or other?
Nick: Okay. Other.
Jack: Okay, explain "other."

Nick: I would say that if you were to take man in the state of nature—as in man devoid of sociality or contact with humans— you'd find that he must act in minimally selfish ways for survival. And with this mankind would exhibit a certain innocence. But I would have to say that this whole question is misguided, because if you judge a man from a state of nature, you're judging him from a state where you've *already* been socialized and can apply those categories to the human you're judging. Whereas the humans who are in that state don't have contexts or labels that correspond or are commensurate with the judgments that you and I are making about those humans to begin with.

Jack: So the problem is sort of like an absence of objectivity?

Nick: Yeah, something like that. So if you say that someone was born with a blank slate, then it's something you're not going to be able to empirically prove. It's just absolutely impossible. And saying that someone is born innocent . . . how can you judge that? It's just impossible. So I would reject that question. That's the first question that I reject logically. It's phenomenologically[3] incoherent.

6. Name two things you consider to be evil.

Nick: Seriously, I would say the pleasure someone takes from someone else's suffering . . . that's evil. Also, acting on behalf of God, while not understanding God on His own terms. I think that violating this principle is the key to terrorist attacks and things like that.

7. How did you decide that these were in fact evil?

Nick: That's probably the deepest question you've posed so far. I would say that in very simple terms it's the phenomenological absence of good. It's a metaphorical space. I guess I'm not really a

---

3. Phenomenology: the study of how a subject constitutes the world from a first-person perspective.

believer in the fact that evil exists, so much as I am a believer that evil is kind of an absence of good, or just a state where good isn't exemplified in any way. So that was kind of a cop-out answer, but that's the one I'll stick with.

Jack: Okay, well this next question might not be applicable then, but . . .

8. How did evil come into existence?

Nick: That's a good question, actually. So, if you're going to go by my logic, it never came into existence. It doesn't have ontological[4] status, because it is just the privation[5] of good. But, maybe you're asking something a little deeper? Maybe you're asking, "Well, how did the privation of good occur?" I'll just say that I can't answer the question that intelligibly, because I don't think there's an ontological status for the privation of something. To say something does not exist, makes no claim as to how it could possibly originate.

9. What gives human beings the ability to reason or think logically?

Nick: Yeah, okay. That's a good question. I like these questions by the way. I think it has to do with an inter-subjective expectation that if we put forth an assertion and are asked to justify our beliefs, we need to be justified in believing what we believe.

And it's a give-and-take thing too where I'm able to understand someone else's justification for their account and integrate it into my own justificatory account. So I would have to say in answer to the question that basically it's the inter-subjective justification that

---

4. Ontological: the branch of metaphysics dealing with the nature of being.
5. Privation: a state in which things that are essential for human well-being such as food and warmth are scarce or lacking.

for any assertion you hold to be true, you have to rationally justify it in some way.

Jack: Okay, so that's what is going through someone's mind when they are thinking logically and reasoning?

Nick: Right.

Jack: So it's something that's innate within humans that allows them to have that mental process?

Nick: Well, okay. So it's not something that is necessarily innate. If it's innate, that just means that we actually know certain things coming into existence. Someone can have a set of beliefs, and none of them are rational or rationally grounded. Rationality occurs in dialogue with oneself and when someone asks you to restate what you believe in a way that has warrant to it. You could also say that it employs the activity of reasoning, which is a more specific application of rationality. Now is that circular, or is it a fair answer?

Jack: I think it's a fair answer.

Nick: Okay, you can gloss it up for me.

Jack: This survey is one of those things where there's no right or wrong answer. Most of the people we ask these questions to have never been forced to answer all of these at once and form them into a non-contradictory worldview. So it's cool talking with someone who has already put considerable thought into them.

10. Where do morals, values, ethics, and standards come from?

Nick: Where do they come from? It's a combination of perspectival interests. What I mean by that is there are certain values that you have in order for you to successfully function in society; and those are the ones that we don't care about as much, but they still add to the picture. There's also a social demand on you to value certain things in order for you to be in conformity with what Nietzsche likes to call the herd. And I don't mean that pejoratively[6], but if you have radically different values from the herd, a lot of times they have places for you to go . . . like jail or an institution. I think our values are not only dictated by certain personal and social expectations but also are largely grafted onto conformity. Unfortunately.

11. Is there any truth that is absolute? If yes, give two examples.

Nick: No, there are no examples of absolute truth, because absolute truth requires it to be true from no perspective whatsoever. Or it's a perspective from every perspective. The only entity that could possibly succeed . . . that entity would be something like God.

But as far as humans are concerned, we have a perspective that we work from, and that perspective has the very limited range of our experiences. And we can never contain what I like to call a synoptic view, which means an overall view of things. We piece together certain bits of knowledge in order to understand their inter-relations; we try to understand them holistically, but we can never succeed in identifying everything as a part of the whole that it instantiates[7]. So we have just a limited capacity for "absolute." Now when you're asking about absolute truths, you're saying, "Give two examples where there are absolute truths," right?

Jack: Yes.

Nick: So one absolute truth is that there is no absolute truth, and I guess the second would be that the only absolute truth that could exist would be that of God. Hopefully I didn't cop-out on that question.

Jack: No, I don't think you copped-out.

Nick: The questions on here are excellent. They're interesting and meaningful.

---

6. Pejoratively: expressing contempt or disapproval.
7. Instantiates: represents as or by an instance.

Jack: Okay, I'm glad to hear you say that. And I like that in saying there isn't any absolute truth, you recognize, unlike many people, that the statement, "There is no absolute truth," is an infinite regression.

Nick: Absolutely.

Jack: If someone answers, "There is no absolute truth," the next question for them would be, "Is the statement you just made absolutely true?" And so on to infinity. Okay, next one. You're almost done. You're hitting the home stretch.

Nick: I could go on for hours.

Jack: Well, maybe I'll make up some bonus questions just for fun.

12. Is there anything real besides what our five senses tell us? If so, how can you know it is in fact real?

Nick: This is going to be another one of those outlandish answers that maybe you'll find suspicious. Okay, everything is real. Everything that we touch, taste, smell . . . our hallucinations are real.

The distinction I'm making is between something that is real and something that is true. If you go up to a schizophrenic and ask them about their experience of hallucinating a pink elephant, that hallucination is real. It's not something that did not occur. It's just something that doesn't concord with what is truthful.

So my answer would be that everything is taken as real, but very few things, namely our statements and judgments *about* reality, are taken as true. And truth essentially indicates a certain structure to reality that reflects a state of affairs that would occur through every individual's perspective, if they were perceiving and thinking correctly.

13. Which of the following best describes your view of God?

1) Creator of the universe but no longer involved

2) Creator of the universe and still involved in the affairs of
humans
3) Not the creator but the essence of all that exists
4) If none of the above, give a brief explanation

Nick: Without a doubt, number two. Just to briefly go through
the examples: number one is having a god that has no personal
importance in your life. If He does, it's just on a very derivative
level. He just created and put everything in motion, but you can't
really have a personal relationship with Him.

The third choice basically means, if we understand the
structure of reality through the essence of things, we understand
the truth of it. And I want to say that one's personal relationship
with God occurs in a dialectic of revelation and concealment, and
this involves truth, but it's something that even transcends truth.
It's something that has to do with the *meaning* of truth. That answer
has to do with maybe a Socratic or a Platonic type of inquiry, and I
think that at root it's kind of empty.

I'm not a Christian, but if I were a Christian, I'd want a God
who I'd be able to engage with on a personal level . . . at least a God
that has efficacy in my life. I think that would be the only God that
would matter in our existence.

Jack: Just to clarify, that's the kind of God you believe in, or if
you believed in a God that would be the kind of God you'd believe
in?

Nick: That's a good clarification. I'm in a really in-between
state to be honest. I am not an atheist. I'm not even an agnostic. I
just can't call myself a full Christian, because of my values and my
practices . . . I don't go to church, I don't read the Bible . . . if I am
a Christian, I'm kind of a pathetic Christian. I don't put time and
energy into my faith, but I would say that if I were to accept any

notion of God, it would be the God that you mention in part two. It's more of a conditional, than it is a, "Yes, I believe that."

14. What shaped your belief or understanding about these things?

Nick: I hate to go to the whole nature vs. nurture debate again. "It's *all* how I grew up," or "It's *all* in the genes." That's a very dispositive type of mentality that I tend to reject.

Jack: I usually shy away from superlatives too. They make me uncomfortable.

Nick: Yeah, I'm with you on that, Jack.

15. What would be the chief purpose of man (individually & communally)?

Nick: Alright, let's just go with the community first. In the community, I think you have to be not just an upstanding member of your ethical community, but you also have to be an exemplar for an ideal that a society would strive for. It's not enough that we obey the law, or that we're good citizens. It's about pursuing projects that are motivated by and lead to the progression of the individual and society.

On the individual level, you may think this is strange, and I'll have to explain myself, but I would say it's the process of self-deification. That essentially means we have our perspectival values and try to come up with projects where we become who we are. It's the idea that you channel all your efforts into projects that result in self-overcoming, as Nietzsche would say. This doesn't mean we become who we are in a final sense, because then we'd cease to become who we are. But it involves goals, aims, and purposes.

Now, within that project, there's room for God. There's room for your personal relationship with God. The only difference is the goal in the projects you pursue to overcome yourself, in order to perpetually make yourself a better person, is going to be rooted in a faith in God. It's going to be rooted in the way that you and God coextensively bind together to accomplish those goals.

So I think for both of my answers, I want to say that socially or personally the ultimate purpose would be setting exemplars or ideals that societally or personally would be unable to be reached but should be set out anyway.

Jack: That's good. To sort of restate what you said on the individual level, it's almost like trying to understand God, what His goals would be and joining Him in achieving those goals. And therefore doing something that is outside of yourself and transcending yourself?

Nick: This is where you might disagree with me. You could say that your goals are correlative with God's in the sense that the way you structure your values is going to be dependent on the way He wills you to structure them. Or you could say the very submission of your will to God does not involve you participating in the goals and values of God, but it's a participation of your perspectival interests and values and so forth that perfectly coextend with the will of God.

And this is what I see with many Christians: They say, "Well, all I want to do is the will of God." And what I find lacking there is a real sense of personal motivation to "get ahead in the world." Not materialistically, but to set serious goals for yourself, where you're constantly overcoming yourself. And that "overcoming yourself," I think, is just a developmental progression of the result of you submitting your will to God in the first place.

Jack: Yeah. That makes total sense. Semantically it's a little different, but in the New Testament, Paul talks about dying to yourself daily . . .

Nick: Oh . . .

Jack: . . . everyday you consciously make the choice to die to yourself and those selfish interests and put the interests of God ahead of your own. It means your interests kind of turn into doing things in line with God as an extension of God.

Nick: I would say that's exactly how I would conceptualize it. And I think you might have put it into better words for me. So in my answer, if you could reword it in the way that you said it, that might actually make me look better.

Jack: Well, they aren't my words. They're Paul's.

Nick: Well, I guess I owe something to Paul now.

Jack: Who knew, huh? Well, we're at the last question now. This one's always fun to ask people . . .

16. If your views were wrong, would you want to know?

Nick: Absolutely. Yeah. I would have absolutely no qualms about it. If I were to find out tomorrow that my whole web of beliefs were an error, that's something I'd want to fully accept, because as somebody interested in philosophy, I'm really committed to the truth. And I think that the very recognition of error usually has some correlate in the direct admission of truth. If we're in error about something, and we understand why it's an error, then in some sense we have already understood something truthful about that error. So I don't think it would be something psychologically damaging. It would be something I would willfully accept.

Jack: That's good. I feel the same way.

Nick: Well good. Have you asked anyone and had them say, "No."?

Jack: Well, that's kind of the normal response.

Nick: Oh is it? Okay.

Jack: For me, I'm like, "Well, yeah I'd want to know. Why

wouldn't I want to know everything I'm believing in is wrong?" But some people get offended when I ask them that question. There's this attitude of, "Well, I already know I'm right, so, no, I wouldn't want to know if I were wrong."

Nick: I understand that mentality. Yeah, you're right, and there are a lot of people here in the philosophy program who would probably answer in that way. And they actually act that way too. Even if you give them textual analysis or proof of the fact that their ideas are wrong, they won't acknowledge it. And I just don't understand why they're in philosophy. It's kind of sad.

Jack: Yeah, it's just so arrogant, you know?

Nick: It's very arrogant and narcissistic especially for a Christian who takes a lot of stock in how truth is revealed and the way truth can be concealed as well. It just seems weird that a Christian would say, "Well I have a belief-system that is just impervious to attack." That seems like the ultimate expression of what you said: arrogance.

Jack: Yeah, and it seems that oftentimes the Christians who act like that are the ones who haven't puzzled through some of these questions themselves.

Nick: That's one thing I like about you and Lael. It's not just about faith with you guys; it's about active participation. You know: reading the Bible, studying the Bible, interpreting the Bible, and making sure your views are a coextension of that. You really give your beliefs a critical analysis. And if you don't examine your beliefs in that way, I don't think you can become an authentic Christian, to be honest. Those were very good questions. I enjoyed that fully.

Jack: Well, good. I'm glad you did. Thanks for taking the time to answer them.

I say goodnight, hang up the phone and sit at the kitchen table in shock. Some of Nick's answers are really close to mine . . . some not so close. I immediately hear a voice in my head, "Your move." I'm sinking in inadequacy, so I do what I know.

I painstakingly type up a transcript of our conversation, take three steps to my bed and plop down next to Lael hoping for a few moments of sleep before classes in the morning. My mind races, and I feel conflicted. Excitement and apprehension course through me in equal measure. I know in and of myself that I'm no intellectual match for Nick. At the same time, it seems like Nick is open to conversation and closer to my way of thinking than I had originally expected. What exactly is my next move?

Finally I decide to ask the only one who would really know. "God, what should I do?"

His answer is surprisingly simple. "Just one move at a time. I'm seeing way ahead of you." A wave of relief washes over me, and I know what I need to do.

Chapter Six

Please Let Me Explain . . .

Small streams of semantic misunderstanding often carve staggering chasms of ideological separation. In order to span those chasms, I needed to write a response to help clear up a few of Nick's misguided assumptions about my motives for believing certain things. Only a few days had passed since my survey with Nick, and I could not rid myself of the sheer surprise several of his answers had given me.

For the next week and a half, I holed up at Sprizzo, the restaurant Lael waitressed at in Wisconsin, and set out to take the survey myself—highlighting our similarities and differences. I owe a great debt to God and the worldview class at NTBI. The lectures pulled a lot of material from the writings of Francis Schaeffer, James Sire, and other apologists and crystallized complicated ideas into succinct statements and propositions.

I mailed the finished letter to Nick along with a Bible and some chocolate-covered pretzels (courtesy of Lael). When attempting to reach another heart, one must tread every avenue available—even the chocolate-covered ones.

Dear Nick,
Thanks again for taking the time to answer those worldview questions for me (and on Labor Day no less). I know you wanted Lael and me to write, but I bet you never expected to find divinely inspired writings with an escort of sweets. Then again, maybe you did.

I included the Bible, because I've used quite a few references when backing up my assertions, and I thought you might find it interesting to see what the Good Book, itself, says on various issues. So please accept this slightly used Bible as our gift to you (we thought the distressed leather best fit your scholarly persona).

I don't have all the answers; I don't think anyone truly does. But you said quite a few good things, and some of your answers surprised me, because they correlated so closely with answers supported by the Bible.

I guess I realized that in all of our previous conversations, you never volunteered precisely what you thought about some of those issues—at least not in the detail brought out by the survey.

I could be wrong, but a few of your answers led me to think that you might be misunderstanding a few of my positions on some of the questions. Allow me to place my posterior in the hot-seat and run through the survey, so you can see exactly why I agree or disagree with your answers. Also, I hope to show how the Bible supports my conclusions or has helped me reach them. Most importantly, this isn't meant to finish a conversation, as much as it is to spur our dialectic forward. I want your feedback.

On the first question about how human beings originated, I completely agree with you and want to attach a few labels to what you said. I believe there was a prime mover (God) who engendered beings in His likeness. Genesis 1:26 reads, "And God said, 'Let us make man in our image and after our likeness . . .'"

I also agree with your answer for the second question. There is a purpose for humanity that must contain personal, social, and divine elements.

In my opinion, however, everything must begin at the divine level, because as one gradually learns more about the triune God of the Bible and aligns his or her purposes with His purposes, they begin to actually experience fulfillment on a lasting level both personally and socially. If God originated everything, then all purpose must emanate from God. Endeavoring to create one's purpose solely on the personal or social level never leaves anyone truly satisfied.

I differ with you a little on the third question about what happens after a person dies. Yes, our souls do not die and are eternal. Here's the difference: I think our souls are individualized, and go to be with God, but will receive new "glorified bodies" at the resurrection when Christ returns:

"Then will appear in heaven the sign of the Son of Man, and then all the tribes of the earth will mourn, and they will see the Son of Man coming on the clouds of heaven with power and great glory." (Matthew 24:30)

I don't know if the following will make sense or not, but here goes: I believe that when you believe in Christ, you're not just "inviting Him into your heart." Instead, He becomes your source of life. The Holy Spirit lives in you. While I'm living on this earth, I will still sin, because my sinful nature is still present, even though Christ is in me. I have, in a sense, two sources from which to draw: my fallen flesh or God's Spirit who is living in me. I am no longer held captive by the flesh, but I can choose to submit to it. My eternal position with God (as His son) is never in question, though. I cannot lose my salvation, but I can choose to not grow in my relationship with God. Paul described that ongoing conflict within himself:

"So I find it to be a law that when I want to do right, evil lies close at hand. For I delight in the law of God, in my inner being, but I see in my members another law waging war against the law of my mind and making me captive to the law of sin that dwells in my members. Wretched man that I am! Who will deliver me from this body of death? Thanks be to God through Jesus Christ our Lord! So then, I myself serve the law of God with my mind, but with my flesh I serve the law of sin." (Romans 7:21-25)

Paul was far more eloquent and succinct, than I could ever hope to be. All that to say this: When you die physically, the sinful nature attached to your fallen sinful body is gone forever, but you (your eternal spiritual identity) are still there and so is Christ in you. If your spiritual identity was gone as well when you died, then only Christ would be left, and there would be no reason for Christ to have died for *you*. God desires to continue the personal relationship with you after you die, so if your individuation were not present in your soul/spirit, that personal relationship would be impossible, and the whole purpose for Christ's death would be negated.

Just for fun, there is some far-out evidence of the individuation of the soul in 1 Samuel 28:10-15 where King Saul has a medium bring a spirit back. Spooky, eh?

On the question you rejected logically about whether humans are born inherently selfish, with a blank slate, innocent or other, my answer is on faith, because you're right, I can't really prove it. But it does at least stay consistent with my worldview, which is quite important.

I think humans are born with a sin nature bent toward selfishness. True, it might be as you said, "minimal and necessary for survival," but I don't think humans are born in a state of perfection.

"Adam" is Hebrew for mankind, so when Adam fell, it was in a sense, mankind falling. He and Eve constituted all of mankind at the time, and according to Scripture, Eve came from Adam. If every member of mankind has come from that first fallen man, then everyone is fallen when they are born. It's not a question of fairness. It's a matter of man violating the rules of a completely just God, and God, in His mercy, immediately implementing a plan for redeeming mankind back to Himself. But more on that later. Mankind is fallen in a judicial/positional sense before God as well as in a conditional sense highlighted by our tendency toward wrong action.

I thought your answer on how evil came into existence was pretty creative, but I have to disagree with you. My belief on the existence of evil is based on faith, but I did come up with a logical scenario that might provide an answer to your creativity about evil being the absence of good. Tell me what you think:

I'll use murder as an example. The absence of murder is "living," but the absence of "living" is not murder; it is "death." Murder elevates death to a new status that is beyond the pure absence of a "good" like "living." I would say "evil" is something unnatural and greater than just the absence of some "good." "Evil" is a distortion of a pure antithetical "good."

Adam and Eve did, after all, eat from the tree of "the knowledge of good and evil." Now we have the innate ability to distinguish between the two.

On your answers for where morals and ethics come from, I would have to agree with you and add a little. Yes, we must do certain things to properly function in our society. And yes, society does have an impact on our behavior. But we are not completely bound by our society.

Figures have risen above and critiqued their society from within countless times throughout our history. How else could one explain the evolution of American culture throughout the last one hundred years? If we were really bound by our society, culture would only stagnate.

Paul, writing to the believers in Rome about the moral law God placed in mankind's collective heart, said:

"For when Gentiles, who do not have the law, by nature do what the law requires, they are a law to themselves, even though they do not have the law. They show that the work of the law is written on their hearts, while their conscience also bears witness, and their conflicting thoughts accuse or even excuse them on that day when, according to my gospel, God judges the secrets of men by Christ Jesus." (Romans 2:14-16)

Regardless of how one deals with it, a universal moral law resides inside human beings. My worldview explains this law in a way that is consistent within itself.

On your answer for whether or not there are any absolute truths, I agree with you and would take it a step further. We cannot arrive at any absolute truth on our own and cannot achieve the synoptic or completely cohesive view you mentioned. As you said, God is the only conceivable being who could possibly maintain a synoptic view capable of absolute truth. He is the only one truly outside the box of our reality and, therefore, in sole possession of knowledge that can be deemed truly reliable.

Therefore, God is the only absolute truth and cannot lie. If His chosen instrument for the transmission of His truth is the Bible, the Bible must be taken as completely true. God wants to share wisdom, knowledge, and absolute truths with us through His inspired written Word. From within my worldview, this logic is consistent.

Lael said one of your biggest questions related to God centers on how He chooses to reveal or conceal Himself. Again, from my worldview, God wants us to know Him. He has preserved an ancient metanarrative written by more than forty authors over a 1,500 year period on three continents with one purpose: to show humanity how to begin a relationship with Himself. No other ancient text compares with the Bible in scope, accuracy, amount of historical/archeological evidence, and internal consistency.

My faith rests on His Word, the Bible. The form through which

God chose to reveal His meaning to us has been meticulously copied, compiled, and translated into the Bible I sent you. That transmission process is a topic for another time, but from my worldview, I can be consistent in believing I can know absolute truths by knowing aspects of God through reading His inspired Word.

I can in no way empirically prove to you that my worldview is true. No one can empirically prove the truth of his/her own worldview, because every worldview begins with some sort of belief.

I can show you that my worldview is consistent within itself. I could be consistently wrong, but I haven't found anything in other religions, worldviews, philosophies, etc. with a more attractive level of consistency. Off the soapbox now.

The apostle Peter said, "The Lord is not slow to fulfill his promise as some count slowness, but is patient toward you, not wishing that any should perish, but that all should reach repentance." (2 Peter 3:9)

Here is Paul's no-nonsense explanation about God reaching out through His creation, and mankind's rejection of His authority:

"For the wrath of God is revealed from heaven against all ungodliness and unrighteousness of men, who by their unrighteousness suppress the truth. For what can be known about God is plain to them, because God has shown it to them. For his invisible attributes, namely, his eternal power and divine nature, have been clearly perceived, ever since the creation of the world, in the things that have been made. So they are without excuse. For although they knew God, they did not honor him as God or give thanks to him, but they became futile in their thinking, and their foolish hearts were darkened. Claiming to be wise, they became fools, and exchanged the glory of the immortal God for images resembling mortal man and birds and animals and creeping things.

Therefore God gave them up in the lusts of their hearts to impurity, to the dishonoring of their bodies among themselves, because they exchanged the truth about God for a lie and worshiped and served the creature rather than the Creator, who is blessed forever! Amen." (Romans 1:18-25)

Many wonder at the apparent unfairness of God not divinely revealing Himself to every person, so that everyone has an equal chance to hear about Christ. It is important to keep in mind that the "fair" thing for God to do would be to not allow any of us to be saved. We are fallen. We deserve eternal separation from Him—that would be just. The unfair thing about this entire metanarrative is the fact that Christ voluntarily died for us. That was unfair. The Creator placed Himself in the hands of His creation, to be killed by His creation, for His creation's sake. That is grace. Now, God desires for people to take His good news to those who have never heard, and in many cases we shrink back from this charge. The onus is on us.

I liked what you said about there being something beyond our five senses. Yes, things happen beyond our five senses, but they might or might not adhere to truth, as you said, even if they did truly happen.

My answer goes back to what was said previously. Truth is found in God's Word, and I believe in a literal, historical-grammatical interpretation of it. So I believe in angels, demons, Satan as a fallen angel; in other words, I have a spiritual worldview instead of a purely materialistic worldview. (See Ephesians 6:12.)

I expected your view of God to differ from mine, but you said you would definitely prefer to believe in a god who is presently active in the affairs of humanity. You also said, "I want to say that one's personal relationship with God involves truth, but it's something that even transcends truth. It's something that has to do with the meaning of truth."

I agree, because I believe God is truth and gives truth both its meaning and context. Our relationship with Him is of the utmost importance, because it is our sole source for any truth.

The next thing you said is what I really want to address more than anything else in your whole survey. "I just can't call myself a full Christian, because my values, my practices. I don't go to church, I don't read the Bible. If I am a Christian, I'm kind of a pathetic Christian. I don't put time and energy into my faith."

First, values, practices, and good deeds are not prerequisites. God knows you aren't perfect. I'm not. No one is. No one was able to keep the Law completely in the Old Testament. Outside of the Ten Commandments, there were more than six hundred other recorded commands given to Israel by God. No one was perfect. The Law was given to show man his need to be saved or redeemed.

Paul said, "Now we know that whatever the law says it speaks to those who are under the law, so that every mouth may be stopped, and the whole world may be held accountable to God. For by works of the law no human being will be justified in his sight, since through the law comes knowledge of sin." (Romans 3:19-20) Starting from that premise, you aren't expected to go to church, read the Bible, or even be a good person out of any sense of religious legalism, obligation, or guilt.

Everything starts with realizing our sinfulness. Paul said, "For all have sinned and fall short of the glory of God." (Romans 3:23) So how can imperfect human beings have a relationship with a holy God? To achieve perfection through our own means or good works remains as impossible as ever. Christianity stands as different from every other religion, because at its root lies not what you can do but what Jesus has already done.

Jesus is key. Your personal relationship with God is made possible, by believing Jesus was fully God and fully man, lived a completely sinless life and was thus a perfect sacrifice or atonement for humanity's sin when He died and rose from the dead. When God looks at you, He won't see your shortcomings and imperfections; He'll see Jesus. All debts paid. Legally justified. His resurrection from the dead proved God the Father was satisfied with His sacrifice and showed that Jesus is God and beat death. (John 3:16-18)

So where do the things like reading your Bible and going to church come into play?

Let's say you were falling off a cliff, and I reached out, grabbed you, and saved your life. Would you feel some sort of gratitude toward me? Most likely.

In some cultures (or maybe just the movies) you would run up to me, breathlessly drop to one knee, and pledge yourself to be at my service for the rest of your life. Or you'd at least ask, "How can I ever repay you?" What would your motivation be? I just did something you were unable to do for yourself: I saved your life.

I read the Bible because I'm grateful God saved me from eternal separation from Him. I want to get to know Him better in order to learn about His desires and join Him in accomplishing those desires. I know I'm not perfect. But I know I can do my best to follow His will if I make the effort to better discern what that will is.

Why go to church? Words like worship, teaching, wisdom, encouragement, fellowship, and strategy come to mind.

Worship. Setting specific time aside to put everything away and worship God shows Him that I place value in our relationship. This should happen outside church too.

"I have been crucified with Christ. It is no longer I who live, but Christ who lives in me. And the life I now live in the flesh I live by faith in the Son of God, who loved me and gave himself for me." (Galatians 2:20)

Teaching. Hearing truths from God's Word that will help me, as I try to grow closer to God.

"Follow the pattern of the sound words that you have heard from me, in the faith and love that are in Christ Jesus." (2 Timothy 1:13)

"But the one who looks into the perfect law, the law of liberty, and perseveres, being no hearer who forgets but a doer who acts, he will be blessed in his doing." (James 1:25)

Wisdom. Having more people to bounce ideas off of is always good. If I have a problem, I can seek good advice and support from others who share my worldview.

"The mouth of the righteous utters wisdom, and his tongue speaks justice. The law of his God is in his heart; his steps do not slip." (Psalm 37:30-31)

Encouragement. I can reciprocally offer support to others who are having problems of various kinds.

"Therefore encourage one another and build one another up, just as you are doing. We ask you, brothers, to respect those who labor among you and are over you in the Lord and admonish you, and to esteem them very highly in love because of their work. Be at peace among yourselves. And we urge you, brothers, admonish the idle, encourage the fainthearted, help the weak, be patient with them all. See that no one repays anyone evil for evil, but always seek to do good to one another and to everyone. Rejoice always, pray without ceasing, give thanks in all circumstances; for this is the will of God in Christ Jesus for you." (1 Thessalonians 5:11-18)

Fellowship. I can develop deep friendships with others that could last a lifetime. A friend of mine used this illustration to describe the importance of fellowship: When coals surround each other, they will burn with intensity for a surprisingly long time, but a coal divorced from the rest will cool in a matter minutes.

"So if there is any encouragement in Christ, any comfort from love, any participation in the Spirit, any affection and sympathy, complete my joy by being of the same mind, having the same love, being in full accord and of one mind." (Philippians 2:1-2)

Strategy. Out of those deep friendships, I will be able to partner with others who are like-minded and effectively reach out to the world around myself by showing Christ's love to those who are hurting, endeavoring to meet their needs physically, emotionally, and spiritually. And in so doing, point the world toward Christ.

"For by the grace given to me I say to everyone among you not to think of himself more highly than he ought to think, but to think with sober judgment, each according to the measure of faith that God has assigned. For as in one body we have many members, and the members do not all have the same function, so we, though many, are one body in Christ, and individually members one of another. Having gifts that differ according to the grace given to us, let us use them: if prophecy, in proportion to our faith; if service, in our serving; the one who teaches, in his teaching; the one who exhorts, in his exhortation; the one who contributes, in generosity; the one who leads, with zeal; the one who does acts of mercy, with cheerfulness." (Romans 12:3-8)

Okay, you basically quoted Paul, when you answered and explained the chief purpose of man. You said man's purpose on the individual level involves self-deification in the sense that you would want to learn more about God and then align your desires with His. As you do this, you begin to look more like God. I would say you begin to become more closely conformed to the image of Christ. Paul said, "And we all, with unveiled face, beholding the glory of the Lord, are being transformed into the same image from one degree of glory to another. For this comes from the Lord who is the Spirit." (2 Corinthians 3:18)

You also said that this self-deification is "going to be rooted in the way you and God coextensively bind together in order to accomplish these goals." I think you're right.

In Colossians 3:2-10, Paul talks about dying to yourself. "Put to death" in verse 5 is a continual action in the Greek. We're always working at this with God's help. 2 Peter 1:3-4 deals with us being able to take part in God's divine nature. This thought is in line with self-deification as you described it and not in becoming gods ourselves.

Of course, I agree with you on the last question about wanting to know if my views are wrong. Paul agreed as well. I'll end this letter by quoting what he wrote to the church in Corinth:

"Now if Christ is proclaimed as raised from the dead, how can some of you [believers] say that there is no resurrection of the dead? But if there is no resurrection of the dead, then not even Christ has been raised. And if Christ has not been raised, then our preaching is in vain and your faith is in vain. We are even found to be misrepresenting God, because we testified about God that he raised Christ, whom he did not raise if it is true that the dead are not raised. For if the dead are not raised, not even Christ has been raised. And if Christ has not been raised, your faith is futile and you are still in your sins. Then those also who have fallen asleep in Christ have perished. If in Christ we have hope in this life only, we are of all people most to be pitied." (1 Corinthians 15:12-19)

Trusting in Christ takes faith, but it's not a blind risk.

Nick, I've had fulfillment since I gave my life to God by accepting Jesus' sacrifice for my sins. Life hasn't been perfect. Bad things still happen, and I perpetrate some of them. But I am not living for myself; I'm living for something greater than myself. I have true purpose and thus lasting fulfillment. I'll never be able to empirically prove it, but I can tell you that once you experience that kind of fulfillment, you can no longer deny the truth of its existence.

I love you, man. You have an amazing mind and are an incredibly understanding person. I've met few people who are actually able to graciously put themselves in other people's shoes like you. You're all laced-up and double-knotted; it's inspiring. Far fewer fully disassociate from their presuppositions long enough to actually hear someone else's views and logically weigh them. I have never met a better listener than you.

Jesus often taught by asking questions, so you've already got that going for you. Thanks for your friendship. You've really stretched my brain these past few months, and I look forward to your letter in response.

Your move.

Jack

Chapter Seven

Social Media:
The Informal Decimator of Distance

About a month had passed since I sent Nick my letter. We had talked on the phone a few times since then but were both very busy. I was putting my life on the line teaching drivers' education part-time, while taking classes at the Bible school, and Nick was busy teaching intro philosophy classes as well as working on his Ph.D.

Social media was a brilliant explosion, but I'm not an addict; it's more of a utility for me than a shot in the arm. An instructor once offered some sage advice, "Don't be a slave to technology; make technology your slave." With that in mind, I never chat, because chatting sucks you in and when you look up it's four in the morning . . . a week later. But on one evening, I spotted Nick's name on the chat sidebar, and decided to see if he was there.

He was.

Jack: Hey, what's up man?

Nicholas: Just replying to some friends . . . .

Jack: Are you defending your doctoral dissertation this semester?

Nicholas: Defending the dissertation prospectus, which is a two-hour exam over what your main argument will be in your dissertation. The real defense is in the spring.

Jack: Ahhh, okay.

Nicholas: Most surely :) How have you been?

Jack: I've been well . . . classes have been good. I'm also teaching drivers' ed. part-time, so that's been interesting . . . .

Nicholas: Oh dig . . . any reckless drivers?

Jack: Only a few . . . I have a special way of stopping the car though . . . . I don't have to use it very often . . . .

Nicholas: Yes, the right brake . . . .

Jack: So much power . . . .

Nicholas: Heh, it's Nietzschean par excellence . . . .

Jack: Ha, most of the kids are actually pretty good though. How've things been for you? Has it been tough juggling everything? Teaching, writing, thinking, etc. . . . . not that they're mutually exclusive . . . .

Nicholas: I'm a perfectionist workaholic, but only endemic to Philosophy, so that is all I have been doing. I'll have a couple of weeks now to take it easy.

Jack: Ahhh, well, it's good to have a focus. Are you just teaching the one class or more?

Nicholas: Two. Intro to Philosophy . . . So I have a disembodied soul . . . you do too. How are they individuated?

I was beginning to get used to Nick's not so subtle shifts of conversation, but it could still be a little jarring, when he dropped huge issues like that! But really, that was exactly the kind of topic I needed to discuss with him. For some reason he'd gotten hung up on how any soul could actually have a distinct identity (since souls do not contain any detectable matter). Souls lacking individual identities would be a problem, because it would mean that my soul is not a part of me. Personal redemption would remain an impossibility.

Jack: Ah, here we go, haha. Okay. I'll explain my take from my worldview . . . .

Nicholas: Sure.

Jack: So man is the only thing according to Scripture that is created in God's image . . . "In God's image" I take it to not imply physicality but the presence of something immortal (soul, spirit, etc.).

Nicholas: Angels are not created in God's image? Are angels immortal?

Jack: Angels are immortal, but they have no chance of redemption, because they were all created at the same time. One man was created and woman (Eve) came from man. All subsequent men and women have descended from those first two. Therefore, mankind can be redeemed through a single perfect sacrifice. Christ died for all mankind, because all of mankind's sin can be traced back to the garden. But many sacrifices would be required to redeem all of the fallen angels, who were presumably created simultaneously, and sinned autonomously. They don't have offspring with each other. Adam and Eve produced fallen children, because they themselves were fallen.

Nicholas: But why do angels need redemption? Are they imperfect?

Jack: The angels had free will apparently, because one third sided with Satan back in the day . . . . this is a sidebar though . . . .

Nicholas: Sure . . . . Go on . . . I mean that in an "I'm very interested to hear this" kind of way.

Jack: I know. I'm trying to get my train of thought back . . . lol.

Nicholas: Fair enough . . . . The problem is with the individuation of souls (disembodied).

Jack: All humans are created in God's image, because they have an immortal aspect of some sort. We are the only things on earth like that. Apparently, the angels are immortal and individual.

Nicholas: Yes, good point . . . .

Jack: So, when we die, I believe that our spirit goes to be with God, but that this is only temporary. In the Old Testament, King

Saul, Israel's first king, visits a medium, and she calls up the spirit of Samuel, a prophet who had recently died, and Samuel's spirit had an identity. Remember in my letter I mentioned 1 Samuel 28:10-15. Hope you looked it up?

Nicholas: Oh yeah, my question would then be, "What would the point of enmattering a soul be?" I can't wrap my head around an immaterial spirit having any individuating features—so let's say all our spirits commune with God after death, how could He tell them apart? A funny question of course . . . .

Jack: I think God would be able to tell who our souls are . . . . God is spirit, right?

Nicholas: God can't be a spirit.

Jack: I guess you're right . . . . One would be mistaken to classify God as anything, because He is outside of everything made.

Nicholas: . . . and immanent to everything made as well . . . .

Jack: I would argue that it is a very different thing to say "God is spirit" vs. "God is a spirit." For one thing, the Holy Spirit is God. The Bible says, "God is spirit," in John 4, and I believe the sense of the passage is concerned more with differentiating God from created material beings, and less with trying to pin down the exact nature or makeup of God. Jesus was explaining to a Samaritan woman that because God is spirit, it doesn't matter where she worships geographically. What matters is her spiritual position before God.

Nicholas: I see . . . .

Jack: Okay, so we die and our souls go to be with God . . . until the bodily resurrection (that's when our souls will be given new "glorified" bodies). Because when Christ comes back and sets up His earthly kingdom, we are given glorified bodies to basically reign with Christ . . . .

Nicholas: Right; and that is how Aquinas thinks he gets out of it, but until the resurrection, our souls have no identity, and thus no place in the cosmic universe to exhibit properties, qualities, or predicate any sort of fundamental distinguishment.

Jack: How can we know what the individuation of spirit would be? We have no way of measuring that, but does that mean it would not be possible?

Nicholas: I agree, we have no way of measuring that, no way of saying Hitler's self-subsistent soul differs from mine until this resurrection . . . .

Jack: Agreed. Is it such a bad thing to not be able to explain it?

Nicholas: For a philosopher? YES.

Jack: Haha, you're so conditioned . . . I kid . . . I kid . . . .

Nicholas: I am . . . tacit understanding does not sit well with me. So, what I am bringing up is a stupid point . . . but Aquinas stumbles around it so poorly. I needed a good answer . . . .

Jack: I think it's interesting to think about. I mean, it's also interesting to think about what a "glorified body" would be like . . . . Lewis sort of takes a stab at it in his allegory, *The Great Divorce*.

Nicholas: Do you mean a pure physicality or a dualistic physical/mental thing?

Jack: The Bible speaks of a "glorified body," as a type of physicality we have never experienced . . . Jesus' risen body is the only example of this . . . .

Nicholas: I see.

Jack: It was a body . . . physical . . . but different than any other physicality, which is one reason why He said the kingdom of God was here and not yet here. Jesus basically established the beachhead for this new physicality, but it will be in its fullness in the future . . . .

Nicholas: In that case, in a quasi-physical description, it seems a moot point: the nature of reality for this new kingdom could not be pigeonholed by our categories of reason and demarcations that accompany them . . . .

Jack: Yeah. I don't think you have to dwell on it necessarily, but it does mean that our motivation should not just be to get to heaven and get out of here . . . . We [the church] are supposed to do good things in this world as a way to foreshadow the new creation and kind of rule Christ will bring . . . .

Nicholas: No, your point is that my point has no existential import, and you are right . . . . So let me ask you something else . . . . Why would God let a baby or young kid burn to death in a fire? Needless suffering.

Jack: You said yourself that we lack a synoptic view . . . .

Nicholas: Yes, a regulative ideal. But even in its absence, we cannot call it "that which we know not, nor desire to explain."

Jack: How can I judge God's reasoning?

Nicholas: Well, you can impute certain attributes to it. Epistemically, to have faith in something that you know nothing about is sheer folly . . . . Now God's reasoning, of course, could be so intricate that our cognitive limits can't wrap around it—well, that's a platitude . . . .

Jack: I think God allows what we call bad and horrible things to happen. He doesn't originate them but does allow them, some say He causes them, but I think He has a reason for those things . . . .

Nicholas: Wow, He causes them?

Jack: Only in the passive sense of not preventing them from happening. I mean . . . if you wanted to press it on God, you could—I wouldn't, but one could . . . .

Nicholas: Oh, that is a very weak causal notion. I see . . . .

Jack: I agree with what you said about the intricacy of God's reasoning.

Nicholas: He is without a hermeneutical[1] horizon . . . .

Jack: Nicely put.

---

1. Hermeneutical: concerning interpretation, especially of the Bible or literary texts.

Nicholas: But go on . . . .

Jack: Maybe that's why I get something new and deeper out of passages in the Bible I've read before?

Nicholas: Why is that?

Jack: When I'm ready to see a truth, I see it, even though it's been there all along.

Nicholas: Obviousnesses do not dissimulate[2] conflict; they foreground them—the question is, "in what way?"

Jack: So what have you been thinking about lately other than burning babies?

Nicholas: I gave a lecture to the grad students a couple days ago on metaphysical holism . . . .

Jack: Did they get it?

Nicholas: I might as well have been talking to a tree. In fact, that would have been more enjoyable . . . .

Jack: Haha, it should make for an easy defense for your dissertation, if no one gets it, right? What conclusions have you come to? Do philosophers come to them?

Nicholas: My dissertation thesis is original—and ambitious, but thorny . . . .

Jack: That is quite an accomplishment . . . .

Nicholas: I spent a whole summer and came out with nothing. I love talking Christianity, because in subtle ways, it is deeper than philosophy.

Jack: In what way(s)?

Nicholas: Philosophy for me, as I practice it, is full of our projection of conceptual hardwiring and abstract language games.

Jack: Hmmm . . . yeah, I see what you mean . . . strange ways of talking about the obvious . . . in ways that are not so obvious . . . .

---

2. Dissimulate: conceal or disguise (one's thoughts, feelings, or character).

Nicholas: But I shun philosophical ethics, which I think is the domain of religiosity.

Jack: Have you read that Bible I sent you?

Nicholas: Cover to cover? No.

Jack: I just wondered if you cracked it open . . . .

Nicholas: Dude, a very nice gesture and well-articulated response. Thanks so much

Jack: Thanks; I can't wait for your response. You're more articulate speaking, than I am writing.

Nicholas: I don't think so. You do have a Socratic modesty . . . .

Jack: Oh, stop it . . . though that might be the nicest thing anyone's ever said to me. That would have impressed me though, had you read it cover to cover . . . .

Nicholas: I took a look at some passages in Revelation, but I have been ensconced in Plato . . . . Do you get a title after your schooling? Like "Sage Jack?"

Jack: Haha

Nicholas: I mean you are studying a lot . . . .

Jack: Bachelors of Intercultural Studies

Nicholas: I see . . . unfair . . . Sage would be better

Jack: I'm not in it for the degree, I guess, but the knowledge is nice . . . .

Nicholas: You deserve more lofty titles, but titles bore the hell out me anyway . . . .

Jack: If "Sage Jack" stuck, I think my Aristotelian piety would wane . . . so where are you at with all this stuff?

Nicholas: What do you mean?

Jack: . . . from the letter and such . . . don't spoil the response or anything, I know you keep things pretty close to the vest . . . .

Nicholas: I plan on typing you responses to your responses after next Wednesday.

Jack: Cool

Nicholas: I will be as ruthless and forthright as possible, because truth always tastes like honey, and the meaning of truth is like the force of using an atomic bomb to disperse a flock of birds . . . .

Jack: I think Solomon said that? Or something like it . . . .

Nicholas: Who was Solomon?

Jack: David's son, and king after him . . . wrote Proverbs, Ecclesiastes, and Song of Solomon . . . wisdom literature of the Old Testament

Nicholas: Could you sum up his wisdom in a terse or epigram?

Jack: Hmmm . . . every pursuit is meaningless apart from knowing God . . . that would sum up Ecclesiastes. He wrote that late in life, after leaving God out of the picture, seeking satisfaction in everything under the sun and finding that nothing gave him true peace of mind . . . .

Nicholas: Is this to say that nothing in the world has existential worth independent of attempting to know God?

Jack: The idea is knowing God and then knowing His desires and joining Him in those desires . . . thus having true fulfillment. You care about what He cares about, in a sense . . . .

Nicholas: I have to go—my grandparents are calling me in German. I will write you soon, before I've taken too much time off my clock.

Jack: Haha, alright. Take care

Nicholas: It's been my pleasure.

Jack: Mine as well.

Nicholas: Keep doing what you're doing . . . .

Jack: And you keep thinking . . . and get some sleep . . . .

Chapter Eight

Concerning Burning Babies

As you probably noticed, Nick brought up the problem of evil in our chat, and I really gave a dodgy response. In case you're unfamiliar with it, the problem of evil usually goes something like this:

God is all-powerful.

God is wholly good.

Evil exists.

Therefore: God is not all-powerful or not wholly good.

This problem is a logical fallacy called a false dilemma—a fact I was unaware of at the time. Essentially the problem is trying to force you to pick from two options: God is not all-powerful or God is not wholly good. In reality there are more options to pick from. The problem is that even though you can get God off the hook in regard to trashing His goodness or power, you still have to deal with evil's existence.

I'll borrow my favorite example of this fallacy from a friend. Let's say Lael walks up to me and says, "If you love me, you'll buy me chocolate." She's cleverly forcing me to commit to one of two positions: either I don't love her or I buy her chocolate. But there are more options, right? Maybe I bought her chocolate but got mugged on the way home. Or maybe I bought her something else to show her I love her . . . like a gym membership (not recommended!).

Nick narrowed down "evil" to something he termed "needless suffering" or things we might consider "freak accidents" that weren't the direct cause of evil choices intentionally made by people—

things like natural disasters, house-fires, cancer, etc.

This question is extremely prevalent in our culture. For example, the band, Monsters of Folk, portrays the problem pretty accurately in their song, "Dear God (Sincerely, MOF)."

Dear God, I'm trying hard to reach you.
Dear God, I see your face in all I do.
Sometimes it's so hard to believe in.
Good God, I know you have your reasons.

Dear God, I see you move the mountains.
Dear God, I see you moving trees.
Sometimes it's nothing to believe in;
Sometimes it's everything I see.

Well I've been thinking about,
And I've been breaking it down without an answer.
I know I'm thinking aloud, but if your love's
Still around, why do we suffer?
Why do we suffer?

Dear God, I wish that I could touch you.
How strange sometimes I feel I almost do,
And then I'm back behind the glass again.
Oh God, what keeps you out it keeps me in.

Well I've been thinking about,
And I've been breaking it down without an answer.
I know I'm thinking aloud, but if your love's
Still around, why do we suffer?
Why do we suffer?

After sleeping (or laying awake in bed, rather) on this problem of needless suffering, I was still at a loss for a succinct, scriptural explanation worthy of Nick's weighty scrutiny. I was also not content to just chalk the problem up to "Oh well, I guess God's ways really are higher than ours . . ." like I did in the chat.

Then in the middle of Pentateuch class the next day, my instructor sparked a train of thought that led to an answer of sorts. I was so excited to have a response that I rushed home after class and banged out the message below.

Hey, Nick,

I was thinking about the "How could God allow babies to burn to death in a fire?" question, and I think I've come up with a more coherent answer than the one from our facebook chat yesterday.

Horrible things happen, because God has allowed Satan to be the ruler of this world. It's Satan's kingdom for now. Jesus established a beachhead into that kingdom when He defeated death by rising from the dead. This was in a sense the breaking-in of the "kingdom of heaven" into our world.

Therefore, those who believe in Christ are in a spiritual battle because God has commissioned us to take part in it. And much suffering on earth (apart from fallen creation and what humans as free agents inflict on one another) originates in Satan.

If God stopped all of Satan's evil, we would have no part to play in this battle and would not even know a battle was taking place.

Ultimately, God will completely defeat Satan and all of his evil; but by God's grace, God is waiting and giving humanity the opportunity to make a cognitive decision to join His fight against Satan and spend eternity in His presence.

Matthew 24:14 illustrates the amazing depth of God's grace. It reads: "And this gospel of the kingdom will be proclaimed throughout the whole world as a testimony to all nations, and then the end will come."

The root of the word "nations" in Greek is actually "ethne" and means a people group or ethnic group. God is postponing His judgment on Satan until someone from every people group on the planet has had a chance to hear and choose life everlasting.

In Revelation 5:9, John prophetically wrote about Jesus: "And they sang a new song, saying, 'Worthy are you to take the scroll and to open its seals, for you were slain, and by your blood you ransomed people for God from every tribe and language and people and nation.'"

So according to that last verse, someone from every people group on the planet will accept God's message of grace through faith in Christ. Lael and I are doing what we're doing because we want to take this message to people who have no way of hearing and making that choice. We want to join God in what He is doing.

All that to say this: bad things will continue to happen on earth until God completely takes Satan's kingdom from him. Until that time, we must try to understand God's grace in delaying His final judgment of Satan and giving more people the chance to hear about Jesus. I don't know if that makes sense, but I think it's more coherent than yesterday's response.

I love you man and can't wait to hear from you.

Take care,

Jack

As soon as I sent the message, I had this agonizing feeling in the pit of my stomach. What would Nick have to say? Was my answer good enough? Mercifully, I didn't have to wait long for his response.

Jack,

While that answer is fine so long as it is confined to, or invokes, the efficacy[1] of Satan, it is always a murky issue as to the extent of God's versus Satan's efficacy in this world. Your appeal to God's grace is not felicitous[2] here, because God's grace only plays a formative role when a sin has been committed and not when needless suffering occurs.

Maybe God's grace will allow for this suffering to be amended in some way post facto, but my question is more trenchant than positing the sources (putatively Satan) and/or aftereffects (presumably God's grace) of needless suffering. My question is ontological: Why does needless suffering exist? It smacks against any teleologically-minded[3] rendition of the "Good vs. Bad" saga. What purpose does it serve?

Even Satan is not concerned with needless suffering! For Satan, I presume, wants us to lead a life in reaction to God and His core values, thus adopting a mode of living that stands for everything God is opposed to, specifically making the choice or aiming at that form of life. But how does the needless suffering of a baby, an entity unable to make such choices, to join the ranks of satanic forces, in any way reinforce or perpetuate satanic intent?

Now maybe Satan's intentions are just as intrinsically perplexing as God's, and in some sense, we would have to presume this. But at the root of it, we cannot even suppose a rationale that would comport with Satan's doings.

In fact, I would hesitate to call the burning of a baby evil, because good vs. evil is a moral distinction, whereas good vs. bad is not. So the burning of the baby is bad and categorically not even

---

1. Efficacy: the ability to produce a desired or intended result.
2. Felicitous: well chosen or suited to the circumstances.
3. Teleologically-minded: the explanation of phenomena by the purpose they serve rather than by postulated causes.

within the realm of God's goodness in opposition to Satanic evil. It is perfunctory[4]; it is a superfluous feature of the world that cannot be explicated.

So I feel my question has not quite been answered yet, although you made headway and convinced me that my question does have textual address in the Bible and is not something epiphenomenal[5] to it.

Let me ask you a more philosophically-minded question about your faith in opposites. Isn't it in some way necessary that Satan exists? If one believes, as I do, that everything is essentially interrelated, then being someone who is good is inextricably tied to what our conception of bad is.

With the eradication of either, we cannot say that God is an intentional entity, (i.e. stands for a specific nature), because all of the relational attributes associated with the constitution of His identity (namely by being opposed to satanic values). So if it all is good, then nothing is good, because we do not know what it is good for, of, about, etc.

I enjoy conversing with a deep mind like yours Jack—indulge me in foregrounding how badly I have misapprehended these issues!

All the best,

Nick

Reading Nick's response, was like hearing him casually call across our theological chessboard, "Check." My heart didn't just sink, it smashed through the floor and plummeted beneath the strata to some deep underground magma chamber, where it was incinerated and pressured into an infinitesimal lump of coal just

---

4. Perfunctory: An action or gesture carried out with a minimum of effort or reflection.
5. Epiphenomenal: A secondary effect or byproduct that arises from but does not causally influence a process, in particular.

shy of a diamond. In short: I felt at a complete loss.

I quickly retreated from my computer where Nick's response glowingly gloated at me, crawled onto my bed, curled up with one of Eric Larson's exciting works of historical non-fiction and sought to escape any confrontation with my own ignorance and inadequacy. At that moment, I heard God's chiding voice in my head—it wasn't angry; it was reassuring.

He said something to the effect of, "I'm sorry, Kid. Did you think your own intellect was at the root of these responses? It seems you were a bit mistaken, but don't beat yourself up. Now that you realize Who's in charge, let's get on with it."

So I whispered something like this, "God, You're in control. Thanks for choosing someone like me to speak to an intellect like Nick. Your choice of instrument surely highlights Your power. Please give me Your words of response to Nick, because they are beyond me."

Having regained the healthy respect for God's position and Nick's mind, I begrudgingly rolled off the bed and made my way back across the room to my computer. I was still apprehensive but decided to read Nick's message again. And as I read, a response began to unfold in my mind. Thank God.

Chapter Nine

A Beatific Light Bulb

My fingers began to type . . .

Nick,

First off, I love you and your brain! I love the fact that we can talk about these issues. I mean, these questions are the nuts and bolts of belief. I don't think blind faith is healthy, because faith, regardless of its object, contains so many presuppositions that are rarely scrutinized. Many leap first and look later. Not the case with Nick Chapman, and I think that's admirable. Again, I love your thirst for knowledge and truth, and I loved your response!

It's a challenge to coherently answer you, and if by some miracle I succeed, the credit should not go to me. I'll try to clarify a few things, but the distinctions you made were good. This is all very general, so I'll get straight to the response.

I think God's grace is aptly applied to this situation. Yes, God's grace is what a person receives when they choose to believe that Jesus Christ offered Himself as a sinless sacrifice on their behalf (Romans 5:1-6; Titus 3:4-7; Ephesians 2:1-10). I'll make a semantic distinction, though, because I think I spoke a bit of "Christianese" in my previous message. It's easy to let the definitions of religious words like "grace," "salvation," etc. become too loose.

Instead of saying God's grace is involved in delaying ultimate judgment before every people group has had an opportunity to hear, we'll say that His mercy is involved. He is truly a just God, and could justly wipeout Satan at any time whatsoever.

We, however, are the lynchpin. In order to completely redeem humanity as a whole, God has chosen to withhold judgment until someone from every different segment of humanity can be counted as having accepted the grace God has provided through Christ's sacrifice.

Postponing judgment means God chooses not to depose Satan and subsequently recreate earth (in a state of perfection). Needless suffering is directly tied to the fact that earth is in a fallen state. Satan is in control at God's allowance. Needless suffering will cease after God deals with Satan, but that won't happen until representative humanity accepts God's grace.

This brings us to the next topic: Satan's strategy. I respectfully disagree with your statement that Satan is disinterested in needless suffering. The source answers the ontological question. What does Satan hate most? When we accept God's grace through Jesus. Satan knows his rule hinges on us remaining firmly under his control. What does needless suffering cause humans to do? For many it is the single largest obstacle between them and God. "How could God allow this to happen to me?" "Why would God do that to them?"

Of course Satan loves needless suffering! It serves his needs quite well by discouraging belief in God, or the desire for a relationship with a God who would allow needless suffering to occur. Satan almost never gets the blame, because he has largely succeeded in his greatest trick, right? Many who even believe in the existence of God, consider Satan the stuff of fairy tales. That's just how he'd like it.

Here's Satan's advantage: he doesn't have to get you to become evil; he just has to keep you from believing in a loving God and accepting God's grace through Jesus. If he can make you cynical or question God's goodness through something as common and overarching in our fallen world as needless suffering, then he can cross you off his list of susceptible, high-risk humans (I doubt Satan really has a list of that sort, but you know what I mean . . . you cease to be a priority if you dismiss God right away because of needless suffering).

That's why Satan has worked to make needless suffering pervasive in our world. Obviously, he also influences humans to carry out his worst atrocities whenever he can, because that is like a smack in God's face, saying in essence, "Look how far I've convinced Your creation to rebel against You."

My point is that needless suffering is in fact a tool of Satan and therefore not "needless" by his standards. In Job's case, Satan had permission to cause horrible things to happen (Job 1:12; 2:6-7). In fact, the book of Job is a clear example of Satan using "needless suffering" to tempt someone to doubt and curse God. Satan did not succeed in that instance, but I fear he succeeds all too often today.

If Satan effectively keeps people from even classifying needless suffering as evil, then he remains even more disguised, and God still receives much of the blame and doubt from his human creations. Did Job's "friends" ever blame Satan for Job's trouble?

The truly sad part is that God loves us all so much, and patiently endures our insubordination. God endures because He doesn't just want some of humanity, He wants all of it. Otherwise, the perfect humanity exemplified in Adam and Eve would never be re-realized. Again, remember 2 Peter 3:9 says, "The Lord is not slow to fulfill his promise as some count slowness, but is patient toward you, not wishing that any should perish, but that all should reach repentance."

God desires all of us to turn to Him and have a relationship with Him, so He waits on us. How merciful is that? It's love that truly is like 1 Corinthians 13. Read that chapter to get an idea of God's love. It's amazing and hard to believe, but when you accept it, nothing compares.

I was thinking about your paragraph about needing evil to understand good. At first I thought it was moot in light of what I wrote above, but now I see your point. It seems that angels were created in a state of perfection, with free will, but were also in the direct presence of God. It's unclear how long Lucifer served God, before he rebelled and convinced one third of the angels to join him. Before that rebellion, we were not around, and apparently there was no need to know anything other than God. What would be the point? If you could truly know God in His presence, I'm sure you'd conclude that God is better than good. God is best.

Lucifer's rebellion might have brought knowledge of good and evil to the rest of the angels, but apparently he was the first to rebel. How he decided that rebelling was an option in the first place, is in my opinion, unanswerable and unfathomable (Adam and Eve were sinless and walked with God and chose to rebel, albeit after Satan tempted Eve). We are told that pride was the root. I can't imagine being in the presence of God and wanting something more.

Yes, God can exist as good in the absence of evil, because He is the essence of all that is good. We define good because of His existence, not because of evil's existence. I think Satan (Lucifer) was created at the beginning of time when God created the universe. I believe Satan fell sometime after Genesis 1:1, but before Genesis 1:2. In Job 38:6-7 we see that the angels were present and watching as God created the earth. Tangential/speculative topic, but important nonetheless.

Nick, I love talking with you. Responding to your thoughts necessitates much prayer for wisdom on my part. It blows me away, and I'm honored to call you my friend.

Jack

I asked Lael to take a look at the message, and she gave it her stamp of approval—after finding a few typos. I clicked the send button, and peace settled over me. How could I have doubted God's provision—paralyzed by fear—a few moments earlier. I said a quick prayer—thanking God I hadn't been checkmated and asking Him to continue working on Nick's heart.

Nick's surprising response arrived that evening.

Jack,

I certainly appreciate the time and effort you put into these replies—and, as always, for your kind words. I also am beginning to realize more and more that your cognitive depth is a challenge and a reward.

Your argument regarding Satan's desire for needless suffering was positively cogent. What better way to question God than to have unexplained evil? In a way, I would revamp my argument to say exactly the opposite of what I was attempting to explicate: Satan predicates himself on evil without a determinate source, for if everyone really knew that Satan was evil and the principle of suffering as it were, then incontinence of the will aside, everyone would shun him. But it is precisely evil, whose modality is such that it could possibly have been engendered by God, that Satan seizes on—a very nice refutation of an idea that I didn't work through to its end.

Your friend,
Nick

Nick's response completely surprised me. This was the first time he had truly and unapologetically agreed with a contrary position of mine. I couldn't believe it. Honestly, it was further evidence that God had helped me answer Nick's response, and that God was working on Nick's heart. I shot Nick a message back.

Hey, Nick,

I put time and effort into these conversations, because I actually do care about you. I hope we can continue to develop a strong friendship, because you aren't the quality of person one runs into everyday. We can converse about topics that have great meaning, and even though we sometimes differ in major ways, we're still able to discuss them and have mutual appreciation for each other's views.

Even if I had a friend with whom I could discuss these things, it is unlikely they would be able to do so with your degree of openness and acceptance. You never get upset or irritated and are willing to re-explain yourself if need be. I greatly respect your intellect, and honestly hope that at some point you might know exactly why I have chosen to believe in Jesus.

I can't wait for your response to this or my previous letter, and I hope that everything with your defense goes well.

Oh, I was wondering, and this might not be the right medium to talk about it, but I'm curious as to whether or not there is anything you've experienced personally that has made this issue of God's relation to needless suffering especially important to you.

Can't wait to hear from you,

Jack

Chapter Ten

"How Could God Allow Suffering?"
she asked

Back in Wisconsin, Lael and I were still plugging away at our biblical studies. I was still putting my life on the line in the driver's ed car, and gradually perfecting my northern accent—Lael's was better than mine. She's quite the linguistic chameleon! Nick and I still talked on the phone from time to time, but then one day he emailed me with an interesting request:

Jack,

Again, I appreciate the kind words. Ninety-nine percent of the time I come across Christians it is a frustrating endeavor for this reason: their lack of reflectivity. What is said in the Bible is such, and they stand by it unflinchingly. But they forget that exegesis[1] and hermeneutical recovery is pivotal in rendering any notion of biblical doctrine coherent; that genuine self-reflection over one's personal relation to God is a necessary but insufficient condition for the establishment of a good ontology[2] and epistemology[3]. And lastly that there can be no dialogue or conversation with this attitude, or something like any meaningful discourse. Without doubt, such a man has no faith.

Your complements work conversely: you are also open and tolerant enough to hear out people's ideas (my crazy ideas for one) without pre-conceived prejudices, while still maintaining

---

1. Exegesis: critical explanation or interpretation of a text, especially of Scripture.
2. Ontology: the branch of metaphysics dealing with the nature of being.
3. Epistemology: the theory of knowledge, especially with regard to its methods, validity, and scope.

a strong self-attribution, i.e. what you really stand for. You are not recalcitrant[4] in the least, and I feel your sustained efforts in maintaining a dialogue with me flattering. As I continue to explore Christianity, I too might find it revelatory and something I'd want to commit myself to. Right now, I do not have strength.

About needless suffering—no, it is not a topic germane to my situation. Just an off-the-cuff thought-experiment.

I have a task for you! One of my students is very interested in needless suffering and is an ardent Christian, but she does not know what from the Bible she needs to read to direct her.

I said, "I know just the guy!" If you could tell me passages that would be helpful to her, I'd be much obliged.

I defend tomorrow, so pray for me! Toward the latter part of the week, I will respond to all your queries in full. Hope you are doing well; it has been a distinct pleasure. Tell Lael hi for me.

Best,

Nick

I was in complete shock. Here was Nick—an unbeliever—asking me to help his student—a believer—to answer one of the most perplexing questions Christians face. I was beginning to see that Nick really was committed to learning the truth. Something was definitely changing in him. I wanted to give his student a comprehensive answer, so I spent a few days digging into my Bible and a few resources. I wanted to paint a clear, foundational picture of Satan's role and motivations throughout the Bible.

Hey, Nick,

I'll definitely be praying for you to feel at peace. I know you've put in the effort and thought—probably more thought than most.

---

4. Recalcitrant: having an obstinately uncooperative attitude toward authority or discipline.

I'll also pray for clear and concise articulation of your ideas.

As for the task you've handed to me . . . I'll try to order the passages for your student in the order that would make the most logical sense. I think it would be helpful to weave the passages into the narrative I tried to set out in that earlier response.

Here's what I'd say to your student:

Many Christians don't think within a metanarrative, when they're looking for biblical truths. They try to pull out individual proof texts to cover their points, because they see their point as if it were completely divorced from the grand metanarrative of the Bible itself.

Postmodernism has, in effect, destroyed most people's estimation of the importance or belief in general of metanarratives. The Bible must be seen as one, however, or you'll never get satisfactory answers. Or I should say, the answers you get will at best be sterile and academic and lack the full force and weightiness that comes when a small truth is seen in proper relation to the larger context within which it fits.

Here's the outline.

There are more verses on these issues in the Bible than just the ones included, but these should give you a few jumping-off points.

God created everything, including Satan, and Satan rebelled, was sent to earth and granted dominion by God over the entire earth for a time.

- Genesis 1:1– God's initial creation of everything, including Satan and the other angels
- Job 38:6-7– Depicts the angels looking on as God created the earth
- Isaiah 14:12-14– The history of Satan's fall and prophetic information about his demise

– Ezekiel 28:14-17– Same as above . . . both past and future
– Revelation 12:4– One third of the angels followed Satan in his rebellion
– Gen. 3:15– After Adam and Eve fall, God promises to send the Redeemer who will enable humanity to come back to God. God promises that Satan will bruise the Redeemer's heel (on the cross), but that the Redeemer will ultimately crush Satan's head (upon His return). This is one of the most important verses in the Bible, because it references both the turning point and the climax of the metanarrative.

The following verses describe Satan's authority on earth:
– Matthew 12:26– Jesus mentions Satan's kingdom on earth
– John 12:31– Jesus describes Satan as the ruler of this world

The book of Job shows Satan's role on earth in the most complete light. The book could be seen as an experiment by God to unmask Satan's method for using "needless suffering" as a means of drawing humans away from a belief in God or desire for relationship with Him.

In the first chapter of Job, Satan goes before God in heaven, and God says (loose paraphrase), "Oh, hey, Satan, have you seen my servant Job? He's blameless and follows me completely."

And Satan retorts, "Well, Job only follows You because You've blessed him, and he has a comfortable life. If things went south, he'd certainly curse You to Your face."

God had apparently been protecting Job, so Satan asks God for permission to afflict him. He isn't given authority to kill Job, but he does cause a house to fall on Job's kids by what appears to have been an earthquake or some natural disaster. We might see Job's circumstances as needless suffering, if we were in his shoes.

Satan was also given permission to afflict Job's body, so one could say Satan is responsible in some cases for disease as well. Basically, Satan was granted permission by God to afflict someone on earth in ways that we would sometimes refer to as "needless" forms of suffering.

What is Satan's purpose in needless suffering? He wants us to curse God. He wants to keep as many people from desiring a relationship with God as he can. Satan never gets the blame for needless suffering, so it's really his perfect attack. But Job refused to be taken in by Satan's most subtle trick, because he knew the Lord and His goodness.

The more important question is, "Why would God allow Satan to use 'needless suffering' on anyone?"

Think of the problem in this light: The earth is Satan's kingdom, and all suffering not directly caused by man (or fallen creation) originates in Satan. Therefore, the only way for God to completely do away with needless suffering would be to completely remove Satan and his kingdom once and for all (while judging humanity and recreating earth), but God in His mercy has decided that before He will completely deal with Satan, He wants to redeem all of mankind:

- Revelation 20:1-3– Details Satan's initial imprisonment in the future
- Revelation 20:7-10– Predicts Satan's final destruction . . . it will happen
- Matthew 24:14– the gospel will be proclaimed to all nations . . . then the end will come. "Nations" in Greek is "ethne" and refers to every people group on the planet, not geopolitical entities.
- Revelation 5:9– details first the desire of God for all peoples,

tongues and nations to be represented with Him . . . Revelation 7:9 depicts this fulfillment. God gets what He wants.

– 2 Peter 3:9– God isn't slow in dealing with Satan by sending Christ back to earth but is patient with us. He's waiting until humanity has had a chance to accept redemption.

– Mathew 28:18-20– Satan bruised Jesus' heel when Jesus died on the cross as foretold in Genesis 3:15. After Jesus' resurrection, He took authority from Satan on earth, but has not completely defeated or judged Satan yet—that's when the second part of Genesis 3:15 will be fulfilled and Satan's head will be crushed. The bruise is gone and Jesus' heel is ready to crush some satanic skulls! See Revelation 20:7-10. "Death" was completely defeated by Jesus' resurrection, but death and Satan are two different things. Death once held power over us. After the cross, we can accept Christ's sacrifice, and eternal death (separation from God) cannot touch us. That's the power Christ's resurrection took from Satan.

Therefore, God delaying His judgment of Satan and allowing Satan to afflict us with what appears to be needless suffering is an act of God's mercy toward us. God is waiting on us. To put an end to Satan and needless suffering right this instant would also mean the judgment of humanity, before someone from every people group has had a chance to believe in Jesus.

That's why the great commission in Matthew 28 is so important for believers. Cross-cultural evangelism is vital, because as Matthew 24:14 stated, the end will not come until someone from every people group on the planet has heard the Good News. God is allowing us at this time to take part in His mission to redeem humanity as a whole.

We can, in effect, take part in abolishing needless suffering by going to language groups who have never heard of Christ. Until that goal is accomplished, God will not completely deal with Satan, and we'll have to deal with suffering as a part of life in a fallen world. Far from forcing God's hand, we are playing by the rules He set in place. Scripture indicates that God desires people to reach people (see Jesus' words in Matthew 28:18-20 about making disciples) and that every language group will be reached and present around God's throne (see Revelation 7:9).

Remember, though, that "needless suffering" is not needless to Satan. It's his best weapon of misdirection, because it almost always shifts the blame on God.

Nick told me he liked the response and passed it on to his student. A few days later, Nick sent me a message about how his prospectus presentation went. If he passed, he'd be cleared to begin work on his actual dissertation.

Jack,

I defended my dissertation prospectus decently a couple days ago and passed. I am the first one of the Ph.D. students to have passed it, but I sense many of them are intellectually lazy. I am glad that is behind me! I think I can show existential holism in Platonic thought as a way of fulfilling the meaning of epistemic and metaphysical holism endemic to the late Forms. If I can, I will have constructed a picture of Plato that many would not think possible.

Holism offers meaningful distinctions to be made in terms of constitution, or how parts relate to a whole (the attractive feature of dualism), while still maintaining the whole is over and above the sum of its parts (the whole being the basis for monism). Anyway, enough of my bragging. This leads me to some remarks you made earlier to my student. Let me reply.

'Many Christians don't think within a metanarrative when they're looking for biblical truths. They try to pull out individual proof texts to cover their points, because they see their point as if it were completely divorced from the grand metanarrative of the Bible itself."

I hope you caught some of what holism is in my first paragraph, because you are essentially appealing to a holistic doctrine by saying that we cannot know anything, at least fully, in isolation from other interrelated things. And it is only through the synopsis, the overall systematic whole of beliefs, that we can individuate the content and meaning of individual beliefs. And holism need not conflict with contextualism, which is constitutive of a good holism "viewing from a context, with an eye to the whole."

You also said, "Postmodernism has in effect destroyed most people's estimation of the importance or belief in general of metanarratives. The Bible must be seen as one, however, or you'll never get satisfactory answers. Or, I should say, the answers you get will at best be sterile and academic and lack the full force and weightiness that comes when a small truth is seen in proper relation to the larger context it fits within."

This is easy to say, Jack, but as you read the Bible, you collect bits and bits so as to form a more synoptic[5] view of the framework you are working from, let's say Job. But the achievement of these metanarratives is not a reasonable aspiration; rather it is a regulative ideal. Postmodernism comes at it in a completely different way, usually by debunking authorial intent based on the linguistic structures that are ossified and compel us to error as it were.

It is easy to ascribe a holistic stance to understanding, (and,

---

5. Synoptic: taking or involving a comprehensive mental view.

believe you me, I have spent months studying it) but fall back on the odd paradox that nothing can be known (only nameable; not a logos) unless one understands the system of beliefs (that involve identity-dependencies and/or the theories deriving from them) it is part of. And one cannot understand a system of beliefs, unless one is aware of all the individual beliefs that constitute it. At some point, you will have to compromise and argue that maybe in one framework, like music or medicine, can we achieve such mastery.

Now understanding something's role in a context can be irrespective of interrelating the beliefs oneself. I understand certain linguistic expressions in German for example without knowing the whole language, but if I tried to systematically interconnect all propositions in German, the closer I would come to knowing it more fully, and these interconnections would serve as the foundations by which a belief is bound to.

Best,
Nick

After I reread Nick's message a few times, the meaning and problem of holism began to sink in. On my own I could never have a complete grasp of the metanarrative of the Bible. True holism would mean that in order to fully understand the Bible, I would also need to fully understand every verse . . . and vice versa. How could anyone ever hope to achieve something like this? A few days later, I realized a fact that reconciled the synoptic paradox—I hoped.

Hey, Nick,
Congrats on possibly forming a completely original approach to classifying Plato's thoughts and entire philosophy. That's no small achievement!

I've been trying to organize my thoughts on this topic of holism you brought up. You set off so many things in my mind that were at once different yet interrelated. I've been trying to get a handle on all of it . . . again, achieving coherency is my only aim. Here goes:

I completely agree with you; I guess I am espousing a holistic doctrine. But you've forced me to identify the parts of that holism and what exactly the whole itself would be. First, I think Scripture itself is only a piece or footprint of the whole. God is the whole, and knowing His Word means knowing a major facet of the whole.

For an illustration that's common, let's say God is represented by a complete body, and the Bible is represented as an important part of the body like the circulatory system. I can learn much about the body from that system, but I will not know everything about the body. True, the circulatory system is a vital part of the body. So in studying it, I might find out many essential elements or truths about the body's nature. However, there would still be elements of the body to which I would not be privy, no matter how much I studied the circulatory system. In the same way, despite years of study, we cannot figure God out in a complete sense.

I can pull out the heart, dissect it, and learn about something truly vital to the body (as one proof text in Scripture might shed light on the whole theme of the Bible and God's mission). I would still, however, be in the dark about certain other aspects of the body.

I think Scripture is often made into the whole when in reality it is only a very vital imprint of the whole. However, it has to be said that Scripture itself must be studied as a circulatory system and not as a heart and separate veins, arteries, capillaries, etc. If those individual things were studied independently, one would never be able to ascertain the level of importance each truth actually held. So, yes, I agree that contextualism is a necessary element that works in conjunction with a synoptic view of Scripture.

I also agree with you that the achievement of a completely unerring understanding of the metanarrative of the entire Bible is not a reasonable aspiration. The whole, however, is God, not Scripture. There is no way I could ever achieve a true grasp of the synoptic nature of God this side of eternity. I do not think it is even possible to achieve a complete grasp of the metanarrative of Scripture. I have studied it far too little to make a judgment like that.

God's Word truly is living; new men in new times devote new lives to new study and uncover new and deeper insights into truths that have been there all along. Here is the rub: God is still with us today, influencing us, granting us wisdom to understand Scripture, enabling us to catch a slightly more well-focused glimpse of Him and His nature as we study His Word and develop our relationship with Him. That is the only reason the paradox you mentioned breaks down.

We aren't on our own with Scripture; God is with us and can grant wisdom for things we would never grasp on our own. The Scientist outside the cage is whispering to the rats inside the maze saying, "There's a tasty bit of cheese just down that corridor and to the left . . . you've almost got it."

This leads me to say, "No. You could never completely exhaust God's Word and have a complete grasp of the metanarrative." But I don't believe that a truly complete grasp is needed to know enough to join God in what He's doing. There are many truths in Scripture that are clear, and they become clearer as we continue our life-long learning of their relation to the whole: God.

Here are a few quick examples from the Bible of God letting mere mortals peek into His metanarrative thereby enabling them to get involved with His mission. Notice that in all of these situations either Jesus or God the Father is granting the understanding. Self-study might have been involved, but it did not provide the breakthrough:

In Luke 24:13, two followers of Jesus are walking home on the road leading south out of Jerusalem to Emmaus. Jesus had been killed several days prior, and they were completely dejected.

In their minds, Jesus' death was just like that of other men who had claimed to be the Messiah before Him and had been killed. They had been expecting the Messiah to establish His kingdom immediately and overthrow Rome. Hadn't Jesus truly been the Messiah? How could He have been killed? They just didn't understand. The whole chapter illustrates the misconceptions most likely held by all of the disciples about the political role of the Messiah. Flavius Josephus wrote about several false-messiahs who had ignited political insurrections only to find themselves on a Roman cross of their own.

So Jesus, now in His resurrected body, meets these two followers on the road and walks beside them. They don't recognize Jesus as He listens to their concerns . . . .

"And he said to them, 'O foolish ones, and slow of heart to believe all that the prophets have spoken! Was it not necessary that the Christ should suffer these things and enter into his glory?' And beginning with Moses and all the Prophets, he interpreted to them in all the Scriptures the things concerning himself." (Luke 24:25-27)

They had to be told about the connections and prophecies in Scripture, because their culture had held to a mistaken interpretation of the nature of the coming of the Messiah. They obviously were not expecting the resurrection, but once explained, the Scriptures snapped into even sharper focus than ever before.

Jesus was trying to give His disciples an understanding of all that had taken place and how it had been in motion for a great while:

"Then he said to them, 'These are my words that I spoke to you while I was still with you, that everything written about me in the Law of Moses and the Prophets and the Psalms must be fulfilled.' Then he opened their minds to understand the Scriptures, and said to them, 'Thus it is written, that the Christ should suffer and on the third day rise from the dead, and that repentance and forgiveness of sins should be proclaimed in his name to all nations, beginning from Jerusalem.'"(Luke 24:44-47)

That was a very important part of the circulatory system. Jesus just laid out the true purpose for His coming. In my opinion this holism can truly be applied to God, Scripture, and the study of both, but God's continued presence with the believer is the factor that helps span the paradox of relying solely on achieving a perfect knowledge of all the pieces to build the metanarrative itself.

I love this theory of holism and how it relates to the nature of God and the parts He has given us that point to Him. Truly, Solomon was right in realizing that everything is meaningless apart from our striving to know God more fully.

Best,

Jack

The weeks passed, and I longed for a chance to sit down with Nick face-to-face. It was so hard to communicate clearly via correspondence, and I felt like much of the emotion was sucked out of our dialogue. We were definitely transitioning into the end game, and I wanted to play in person.

Chapter Eleven

Back to Fayetteville

Weeks later, a huge decision loomed over me. Some close friends of mine were getting married in Arkansas on Saturday, and I wasn't sure if I should make the trip. I rolled out of bed Friday morning and walked to class—still undecided. While driving twenty-six hours during a weekend was not a welcome prospect, I really wanted to support my friends. At noon, classes let out, and I was still unsure what to do.

While walking up the hill to our apartment on campus, I asked Lael for a little wisdom (being careful to list off all the negatives: sleep deprivation, no time for school work, etc.). Luckily, Lael has never been one to tell me what I want to hear. She looked at me and asked, "Well, how do you feel about making the trip?" That did it. I knew I needed to go. Lael always helps me see clearly whenever my motivations are selfish. Sometimes you just have to go with your gut (or yield to the Spirit!), and my gut was screaming at me.

About six hours into the drive, I thought of Nick. He lived about an hour from where the wedding would take place. I called him up to see if he'd want to hang out Saturday night, and he said that sounded great. After I hung up the phone, I prayed for Nick and our conversation. I'm not one to "heap up" prayers, but I prayed for a long time. I had a feeling that something big was going to happen, but I didn't know what.

I arrived safe and sound in Fort Smith and the wedding was great! Then I drove up to Fayetteville and met up with Nick and some friends at Arsaga's coffee shop. We talked until they kicked us out at midnight and forced us to migrate to Village Inn (for the pie and coffee). We'd be talking about recent movies, until Nick would interject with something like, "So does the existence of good necessitate the existence of evil? What do you guys think?" Conversation proceeded to get serious until it reminded someone of another movie. Everyone showed signs of wear around three in the morning, and I suddenly realized I had no place to stay in Fayetteville. Nick said I could crash at his place.

Nick and I never slept. We sat at the vertex of the right angle his two living room couches formed and discussed deep spiritual issues and some of his emotional baggage until the sun came up. We were entrenched in conversation about the meaning of being a Christian, when Yoshi, Jared's very large black and white cat, screeched like some kind of wild banshee downstairs. Nick jumped up to check on Jared.

A few minutes later Nick returned and blurted out, "I just can't do it, Jack."

"What?" I asked.

"I just don't have the faith for this," he muttered. "I can't do it."

"Well, what is it that's keeping you from having that faith? What's blocking you?"

Nick looked at me and said, "For one thing, philosophy is pretty much my life, and if I make this choice . . . if I choose to believe in Christ, then all of that time I've spent studying philosophy will have been a waste. I'll have to throw it all away," he paused. "I can't do that."

I thought a silent prayer, paused, and a thought came to me. "Nick, believing in Christ won't negate all of the philosophy you've studied. The only thing that will change is your starting point or perspective." I reasoned, "With Christ at the beginning, your philosophical mind will be pretty amazing. You wouldn't need to throw anything away."

Nick thought and said, "That makes sense, but how can I be a Christian, when I still do bad things? I don't go to church or read my Bible . . . I'd be a pretty pathetic Christian."

I reassured him, "Nick, God doesn't expect you to be perfect or cleaned up before you come to Him. If He did, none of us would ever reach that point. God knows we're not perfect, but He wants to meet us where we are. Once we've established a relationship with Him, we'll actually be able to change, because He'll be helping us. You don't need to change before God will accept you. The change comes later, and believe me, it's a lifelong process."

Nick nodded and said, "Okay, but how can I put my faith in something I haven't studied? I haven't read the Bible, so how can I become a Christian?" he questioned. "It would be completely intellectually irresponsible of me."

Good question. I was searching for an adequate response. "Believing in Christ is just a small step of faith, but it does require a huge leap of trust on your part. But think of it like this: I mean, let's say you take this small step of faith by believing in Christ, and nothing happens? What have you actually lost? Nothing. If anything, you'd know there wasn't anything to this Jesus thing, and you'd no longer need to waste your time with studying the Bible. You could cross Christianity off your list. But, if you take this step of faith, and something does happen, then you'll have even more incentive to actually study the Bible. You don't have anything to lose either way. If you never take that step of faith, and Christ turns out to be who He said He was, you'll have lost quite a bit, though."

As soon as I uttered those last words, Yoshi let out a second paranormal screech from the basement, and Nick leapt up to make sure Jared had not ceased to be. A few minutes later, Nick plodded back upstairs, plopped down wearily on his couch and whispered, "I think that might be something I want to do."

I couldn't believe this was happening. Was Nicholas Chapman really about to believe in Christ? Somehow I knew this had been coming, but in the moment, I was almost in a daze. "Well, why don't we just do that right now?" I suggested.

Nick looked at me expectantly but said nothing. He was waiting for me to take the lead, so I looked at him with a raised eyebrow and said, "Nick, you know there's no special ritual or anything. You're a pretty smart guy. Just tell God what you want to do."

Nick knew the gravity of the decision he was making. Glancing up, he paused then whispered in a shaky voice, "God, I believe You created everything. I believe You created me. I believe that I was born as a sinner. I believe that Jesus is the Son of God, and that He died to pay for my sins and rose from the dead, so that I can have a relationship with You. I want that."

Nick tipped his king.

He glanced in my direction and asked with a bemused expression, "Did it work?"

I laughed and in true Lael-fashion answered with a question of my own, "How do you feel?"

"I don't know," he said with a distant look. "I feel like this huge weight has just been lifted off my shoulders. I feel so light. It's hard to describe!"

I couldn't stop smiling! I told Nick that dozens of people had been praying for him, and a look of startled amazement settled across his face as he asked in a sober voice, "For me?" His incredulity was heartbreaking. He paused and added, "I didn't think anybody cared."

We stayed up the rest of the night and talked about the implications of his decision. I related the story of C. S. Lewis' conversion from his autobiography *Surprised by Joy*: When Lewis was a thirty-year-old philosophy professor (and atheist), he went on long, late-night walks with his friends J.R.R. Tolkien and Hugo Dyson during which they discussed matters of God and religion. These conversations gave him "much help in getting over the last stile." I told Nick I was proud to be his Tolkien, even if that was all I ever was.

Daylight forced it's way through the blinds, and as the birds began chirping outside, I realized, ironically, that it was Sunday. I looked at Nick and said, "Wanna go to church?"

He smirked and said, "Yep."

Chapter Twelve

Doubt + Certainty = Normal

I had only grabbed four hours of sleep in the last fifty, as I pulled away from Nick's apartment and began the twelve-hour drive back to Waukesha. Running on a heady combination of joy and sheer adrenaline, I immediately called Lael and told her the whole story. I choked up near the end, and I could tell she was overjoyed.

As I relayed the story for the fourth time to a friend who had been praying for Nick, I was overtaken by exhaustion and my vision blurred. I put the phone down, pulled onto the shoulder and took a power nap. Hours later, when I arrived home, an email from Nick waited for me.

Jack,

I sense something within you, something that utterly defies sanctimony[1]; something that yearns for the harvest. I can't say what came over me the other night (I was giving a confessional). I was concomitantly inspired by your patience, by your general disposition. (You'd make a great psychologist by the way.)

My psychologist back home is a very intellectual Jewish man, and every time we meet (that reminds me, I need to pay that man!) he reminds me that he thinks of me as smarter, like Yogi Bear! He told me matter-of-factly that I would always feel lonely, even if saved! This seems to be true on a couple of different levels and makes my putative admission into Christianity look like a farce.

---

1. Sanctimony: making a show of being morally superior to other people.

There is this problem: I doubt. I doubt what I confessed should have been so. I doubt I am a Christian, or that I have genuine faith. I did more than just feel that night; I had a pure noetic[2] vision of unaltered faith; it haunted and haunts me. It is the scariest thing in the world to me at present, either that or immanent collapse into mental ineptitude.

And immediately, I love the acceptance of others around me—that people actually prayed for me; it leaves me slack-jaw. For me? I remember my ex-girlfriend saying I had the loneliest eyes she had ever seen. But Jack, you know how silly it is to play the tormented (genius) type, and too easy. God is challenging in a way I never thought plausible.

"What is your upshot, Nick?" you ask?

Jack, I don't know! I guess I really exhort you to hold off on letting me enter the celebratory "let the coronation begin" phase of my life, despite my admissions to you that sacrosanct night.

I still do not feel like a true Christian. I probably do not even act like one. But despite the overwhelming doubts that assail me in the quietest of hours—you foregrounded what? That for which no one can deny! And for that I am eternally thankful.

We will talk soon, and maybe you can teach me to be a believer, a true one that is.

Your friend,
Nick

I felt discouraged, but then I began to think about my own Christian life. It's okay to have doubts. It's natural. God always comes through, and even in the midst of Nick's doubt, he still couldn't deny the truth of his conversion. I suddenly felt an overwhelming urge to comfort him.

---

2. Noetic: of or relating to mental activity or the intellect.

Hey Nick,

Man, I can't tell you how good it was to read your last message. I am amazed at the maturity you already exude in your faith. I would have been incredibly surprised if you were not crowded with doubt.

That would have told me two things. One: this new faith was not much of a stretch for you. Two: Satan must be sleeping on the job.

However, neither of those scenarios characterizes your reality. Despite all the doubt you feel, you still could not deny that moment of pure confirmation you experienced early Sunday morning. You had the maturity to stare through the doubt and remember the truth you'd experienced. I'm impressed and encouraged.

Remember the example we have from Abraham. Initially he had the same amount of faith you did. God told him to go, and he went (Genesis 12:4). After that Abraham had doubts and messed up quite a bit—he even told identical lies about his wife—but God stayed the same and always kept the promises He had made to Abraham. Gradually, as Abraham got to know God better, he had confidence in God's perfect faithfulness. His faith grew stronger—to the point that he was willing to obey God, when God asked him to offer his only son Isaac (Genesis 22). We all start in the same place, but we all grow as we get to know God more deeply.

You need assurance. You made a huge leap of faith, and God met you when you did. Now you need to get to know that God with whom you established a personal relationship. I think it's important that you work through these doubts on your own with just you and God. After all, that's whom this relationship is between. As you know, I believe God's modus operandi for revealing Himself to puny humans is the Bible.

That being said, the primary way you're going to develop the relationship between you and God is through reading the Bible.

I always ask Him for guidance whenever I read it. Try reading through Luke and Acts first, because they're written by Luke and will give you a good overview of Christ's life and how the church began. Then you might try John, because out of all the Gospels, I think you'll enjoy his writing style the most.

Also, try just talking to God. Tell Him if you're frustrated or have doubts. It's okay. God is plenty big enough to handle anything you can throw at Him. Ask Him to give you assurance. Ask Him to help you sleep. Ask Him for wisdom regarding your dissertation. This is the role the Holy Spirit plays in our lives. He brings reassurance. Paul said, "The Spirit himself bears witness with our spirit that we are children of God" (Romans 8:16). Tell him you're glad He desired a relationship with you. Just talk to Him.

I'm so encouraged by your faith. Don't get discouraged. God has amazing things in store for you . . . just get to know Him.

Your friend (and brother now!),

Jack

For the next few days Lael and I prayed like crazy for Nick. I wanted him to realize that he had tipped his king to God and couldn't have it back. I hoped my advice would help and wondered if I should have said more.

Then he responded...

Chapter Thirteen

Fact or Fiction?

Jack!

A friend named Melody tried to explain a metaphor or analogy to me for why Jesus' sacrifice was for all sinners, or taking on all the sins of the world—a gesture that I thought had to be metaphorical. But what I am beginning to believe is not that we need to understand Jesus' sacrifice metaphorically or analogically; we can understand it ontologically, namely as a sacrifice involving Christ's actual acceptance of our humanity through the ontological atonement of all sinners.

This way grounds a secure real foundation for the semantic contours involved with His sacrifice through the metaphysical landscape that atonement constitutes. I think now it is a mistake to think Christ's sacrifice can only be understood metaphorically. If it can only be thought of in this way, it is like a shadowy substance that pops in and out of existence, never fully foregrounding its truth (aletheia). So I deeply regret that I might have led you to think this as well!

Nick

After looking up a few of his words, I was glad to see the conclusion to which he had become convinced: Christ's sacrifice really happened some 2,000 years ago in our space-time universe and actually atoned for humanity's sin. God really was working on him.

Hey, Nick,

First, I completely agree with you about the lack of necessity to explain Christ's sacrifice metaphorically. We often resort to metaphor to help explain the symbolism or foreshadowing of His sacrifice, but all that is needed is the understanding that it actually happened: Jesus' sacrifice atoned for all of humanity's sins (1 John 2:2).

You have to believe, like you did that night, that Christ is the Son of God, died for all our sins, and by believing in His sacrifice you can now have a relationship with God. Like I was saying about the Jewish law-court talk Paul employed when talking about this issue—this act of believing and accepting Christ's sacrifice is termed "justification," because it places you in right standing (in a legal sense) with God. It's not because of anything you do morally or the kind of person you are. Christ's sacrifice is the piece of evidence that allows God, as supreme judge, to find in favor of you. Believing in Christ is like choosing to show the evidence in court. If the evidence isn't brought in, the verdict won't change. God looks at you and sees the evidence of Christ's perfect atonement for your wrongs.

The Christian life is essentially made up of three phases of salvation: justification, sanctification, and glorification.

Justification is the bit we've been talking about. Sanctification refers to your Christian life after you've been declared to be in right standing (righteous or justified) with God. Spiritual growth occurs as your relationship with God develops. Your moral life will begin to change—but not all at once. The Christian life is called progressive sanctification for a reason. It's a life-long growth process. We will never reach perfection or "glorification" until Christ returns and gives us new glorified bodies.

Sanctification and justification are oftentimes mixed together and confused by preachers (and even popular writers). Once we are justified, we can never lose our eternal position before God (as one of His children). Paul said that "those whom he justified he also glorified" (Romans 8:30).

However, like I mentioned in that first letter to you, we can still sin as Christians. As we go throughout our day and are faced with different situations, we choose to rely on one of two sources: our flesh or the Holy Spirit living inside of us. If I rely on the flesh, I'm still God's child. Even though I might have to suffer consequences in the here and now for my choice, my eternal consequences have been paid for by Christ—that's true grace.

One helpful way to look at this idea is that there is a difference between our position and our condition. Our position as children of God will never change, once we've accepted Christ's all-encompassing forgiveness. Our condition in this earthly life, however, is constantly changing.

So you, technically speaking, have been justified, and God sees you in the right. Now you're in the process of sanctification, and obviously, this process is different for every person. We all have different areas we need to grow in, and we'll all be growing spiritually in our relationship with God until we physically die.

No one has it all together, which is where the church comes in. Paul spoke of us as a body made up of different parts (with various strengths and weaknesses). We are all supposed to work together and build up each member of the body.

Much love,

Jack

A few days later I talked to Nick on the phone and decided to throw out a hypothetical scenario. "So Nick, I'm in the middle of my undergrad, and I don't know what I believe about whether or not God exists. I haven't met any intelligent Christians who have tried to persuade me to their side. Plus, I'm seeing that atheism has become very popular, and I'm toying with the idea of becoming an atheist. What advice do you have for me?"

There was a pause at the other end of line before Nick spoke in a carefully measured voice, "I would say you should read something that is representative of atheism and tell me if it changes your heart. Tell me whether it actually has strong personal import. If it doesn't do anything for you, then I think you're impoverished in a certain way, which could quite possibly be spiritual. I'd say that would be the litmus test."

Nick continued, "If you really found you could identify with a secular humanism of some sort, then I would say Christianity is probably not for you."

Panic shot through me, as I feared Nick was advocating some sort of relativistic notion of truth. He quickly clarified, "And I'm not presenting that in a way where Christianity is a flavor of soda you pick off the shelf, and we can pursue these different ideologies that all have their own truths. No, I'm not saying that! I think a good test of your faith, or your ability to have faith, would be the way certain schools of thought impact you."

Nick's voice took on a far-away quality as he said, "I got this question from a guy once, 'How has studying philosophy this long changed you?' I really thought about it for a couple seconds and said, 'I'm really not sure how.' It has obviously changed me intellectually. But emotionally or spiritually? I was still hungry for something else." I could hear the realization in his voice as he continued, "I can say I've been through western philosophy, and it still didn't quite do it for me. There was a lack."

After hanging up the phone, astonishment enveloped me. I felt like Nick and I had just finished analyzing our theological chess game, and as I thought through the dramatic changes Nick and I had made in four short months of friendship, God's faithfulness took on a completely new meaning. God showed me that He can use anyone to reach anyone.

God revolutionized my respect for His Word. I've experienced the benefit of continually pressing and searching it for a greater more comprehensive understanding of truth. The Bible is God's truth revealed, and there are things I hold to and have come to believe are true. He desires us to know truth, and Nick revealed areas where my understanding was weak. I readily admitted those weaknesses, and searched out the answers.

Being at ease with our weaknesses, however, is not okay. Using our weaknesses as an excuse to give up is not okay. Being content with, "Well, that's just the way I was raised. End of discussion," is not okay. Turning off our brains with, "I'm not smart enough," is not okay. Chalking it up to "The Lord just works in mysterious ways," is not okay.

God is definitely "without hermeneutical horizon" as Nick aptly said, but He wants us to press into the story. He wants us to dig. To wrestle. To get dirty. He died for us to engage with Him— the sovereign repository of all knowledge and wisdom. He wants us to learn to trust His Word.

My teacher, George Walker, also said that many people are not willing to consider a change in their belief of God's existence or sovereignty, because doing so would necessitate a change in their view of themselves as rightfully in control. Willfully admitting the truth of God's supremacy forces us to place ourselves in our proper position: under Him.

Maybe you like calling the shots in your own life—that's

human. You will never experience freedom until you are willing to say, "God, I choose to accept that You are above me. You know me better than I know myself. You know what's best for me . . . even if it hurts my pride to say so."

Sure, I can tell someone, "All you have to do is believe in Jesus. It's that easy!" And in one sense, that's completely true. But I'd be lying, if that were where I left things. In order for you to believe that Jesus Christ was the One who cancelled your unpayable debt with God and made having a relationship with Him possible, you must first acknowledge that you—on your own and left to your own devices—are in a state of complete and utter helplessness.

That's hard.

That hurts.

That's humbling.

Some aren't ready to make that admission. Some aren't ready to believe.

That's okay; it's a big decision. It was for me. It was for Nick.

In tipping your king, you won't become the grandmaster, but you will meet Him.

It Takes a Village . . .

. . . to write a book. Throughout this entire process, God has allowed so many different people to enter my life and speak words of encouragement, critique, wisdom, and above all else—honesty. The collaboration has been equal parts amazing and stretching, and I wouldn't trade the lessons learned for anything.

Consequently, I have many people to thank, so I'd better get to it. Family first. Lael, thanks for making this friendship with Nick possible and for supporting (and critiquing) me. You keep me from looking stupid, despite my best efforts! Mom and Dad, for your many methods of support—both in this project and throughout the years.

Thomas, for teaching our worldview class at NTBI. "Timely" would be an understatement. George, there are far too many things to list, but I'll go ahead and try. Thanks for reading and offering such crisp advice, for teaching presuppositional apologetics to thirsty students in your "spare" time, for offering wisdom about the field, for friendship. Dave B., for your invaluable publishing insight! Dave M., for creating the platform.

Todd, thanks for your game-changing, chronological vision! BJ, Jeremy, Matt, and Jake, for reading early drafts and giving it to me straight. Adam, for the "Stephen King" wisdom! Dan, for the lessons in logic.

Thanks to everyone at New Heights and Brooklife who has lent a hand! Mark and Marilyn, thanks for always reserving our spot at the chateau! Jim, for the sage advice. Karen, for working your publishing magic.

And Nick, I look forward to many more years of friendship and non-duplicable conversation! May it never cease.

Appendix A

The Role of Suffering in the Believer's Life

This is the follow-up message I sent to Nick's student:

I want to build upon the foundation that was laid in the last bit about suffering. Now that we have a context for the narrative that needless suffering fits into, I want to explore one jumping-off point in particular that is sometimes associated with this issue: how suffering relates to those who are followers of Jesus.

First, to paraphrase C. S. Lewis' words, I believe that God procures the simple evils perpetrated by Satan and mankind and weaves beautifully complex good from them. Look at what Paul says, "And we know that for those who love God all things work together for good, for those who are called according to his purpose" (Romans 8:28). Basically, if followers of Christ are willing to trust God, He will in the end receive more glory from their situation, when He works it out for ultimate good. This does not mean suffering will cease to exist the moment you believe in Jesus; He's not some super-charged lucky rabbit's foot.

So, if we trust God, He will twist the effects of suffering caused by Satan, mankind, and the Fall to bring Himself glory in the best way possible. Oftentimes this view lies beyond our perspective, for His ways are much higher, more fantastic, and intricate than ours. We aren't alone, though.

Even during the beginning stages of the church, in the mid-60s

A.D., believers were struggling with how to think about and deal with the suffering and persecution they were encountering. Peter wrote his first letter to the Jews who had been dispersed throughout the Roman Empire to aid them in understanding the role suffering should play in their lives: namely that of an effective supporting actor, who should never be confused with the lead. Peter mentioned suffering more than fifteen times in his short letter. Here are a few pieces of his sage advice:

1 Peter 1:6-7:

"In this [your eternal place with God as a result of your belief in Jesus] you rejoice, though now for a little while, if necessary, you have been grieved by various trials, so that the tested genuineness of your faith—more precious than gold that perishes though it is tested by fire—may be found to result in praise and glory and honor at the revelation of Jesus Christ."

1 Peter 2:19-25:

Peter illustrated how we should react toward those who bring suffering upon us, by pointing out how Christ responded when He suffered at the hands of people just like us. Peter reminded his readers that they were once lost as well.

1 Peter 4:12-16:

"Beloved, do not be surprised at the fiery trial when it comes upon you to test you, as though something strange were happening to you. But rejoice insofar as you share Christ's sufferings, that you may also rejoice and be glad when his glory is revealed. If you are insulted for the name of Christ, you are blessed, because the Spirit of glory and of God rests upon you. But let none of you suffer as a murderer or a thief or an evildoer or as a meddler. Yet if anyone suffers as a Christian, let him not be ashamed, but let him glorify God in that name."

Notice Peter said to not be surprised when the fiery trial comes upon you. In other words, suffering will happen. Peter ended his letter by exhorting the believers to stay together and support each other through their trials. Next to God, they were each other's best source of comfort and consolation.

Also, James' entire epistle (the earliest writing of the New Testament) was written to early Jewish believers who had been driven from Jerusalem by persecution after the Sanhedrin stoned Stephen, the first martyr.

Here are some possible God-perspectives to think from regarding suffering. Obviously these are not hard and fast rules (I would not presume to know all the perspectives God sees), but I have seen evidence of some of these.

Some people pray for miraculous healing or some other applicable form of instant relief from their suffering. While God chooses this route sometimes (yes, even today), we must remember that His end-goal is receiving as much glory from the situation as possible.

Remember, God wants to bring all men to Himself, so if He can morph one of Satan's evils and elicit glory from non-believers, so much the better. It is better to pray, in my opinion, for specifics, with the caveat, "however, not my will, but yours be done." Praying in that manner does not imply a lack of faith, because Jesus prayed that prayer in the garden the night before He died. James even said we shouldn't necessarily pray for the trial to be over, but for God to give us wisdom as we go through the trial that we might learn all He desires to teach us through the process. See James 1:2-5.

"Why is God waiting so long to relieve my suffering?" Sometimes, by allowing the suffering to persist, say a medical condition, more people in general become aware of the situation and more believers begin to pray. Then if God does bring relief, hundreds or possibly thousands of people can share in the situation and give God the glory He deserves. God's fame spreads even further.

Oftentimes, I think God wants to bring us to the point of impossibility; that place where we are helpless, and in complete dependence on Him. I don't believe this is punitive, but rather preparatory. When you talk to someone who has been brought to this point of impossibility and then experienced God's unfathomable provision, you'll notice something in him or her has changed. A certain peace and confidence comes from experiencing divine intervention. Many times, God uses these people in incredible ways, because their faith in God's supreme control has been strengthened. If you've never trusted God for the impossible, how do you know He'll deliver?

A friend of mine said we have to be able to rest in God. He explained it like this: Whenever he goes on a long road-trip with his wife, she always drives. He'll even sleep, because he trusts her driving so much. He says we have to get to that place in our relationship with God, where we can completely rest, while He's at the wheel and totally trust Him for the outcome of our situation.

This doesn't mean God wants us to do nothing, but it's more in line with our state of willingness to do whatever He might call us to do in any situation—even if it runs contrary to our logic. Sometimes His message might be, "Stop and wait." It's a hard lesson to learn and requires a developed relationship. Thankfully it's true that though we are faithless, He remains faithful.

"What if God never takes the trial away?" I've seen those who have prayed for joy in the midst of a lifelong trial. I would argue that their remarkable testimony of lifelong joy and contentment in the midst of difficulty was a more effective testimony to the world of God's provision than a miraculous healing would have been.

This next point is directly related to the previous. God might wish to refine us by allowing us to pass through the fire. Again, this is not a punitive form of judgment, but a preparation for some greater purpose. If you read the story of Abraham, you will find that he was not a man of faith when he started out. Sure, he initially obeyed God's command to go and leave his homeland behind, but he also faltered in his faith in God.

Toward the beginning of his story, Abraham feared that Pharaoh would kill him, so he could take his beautiful wife Sarah as his own. Abraham lacked faith in God's protection, even after God had promised in Genesis 12:1-3 to bless him and make a nation out of him. He lied to Pharaoh by telling him Sarah was his sister. God never once failed him. God met Abraham where he was and actually blessed him in this situation.

Then twenty-five years later, Abraham found himself in the exact same situation. Keep in mind God had shown himself to be faithful to Abraham all throughout those twenty-five years. So what did Abraham do this time, when he found himself in an identical situation? He told an identical lie. What did God do? God stayed true to His promise of blessing Abraham and delivered him out of the situation.

Eventually, Abraham learned God was completely faithful. Even Abraham, who's mentioned in the "hall of faith" in Hebrews 11, had to develop and grow in his relationship with God. Some interpret this section to be highlighting God's constant faithfulness in the lives of men who weren't always so faithful. One of my teachers told me that when you're reading the story of Abraham, God should be seen as the main character, because He never changes and is always faithful. Remember that.

Sometimes several of these reasons might be at play, when God is allowing us to go through suffering. The end goal, however, might be to help us better relate to another person who later goes through the same circumstance. How many times do you hear of someone coming out of a horrible situation and then establishing an organization to help others who are suffering in the same way? We can be a witness to the fact that God does have everything in control, even if it seems impossible for us to imagine His reasoning. God can use us to help bring hope to other hurting people. Some of these stories in the Bible can have that effect on us too.

In Genesis, you can read the story of Joseph. How many times did Joseph have to undergo suffering? He was sold into slavery by his brothers, wrongfully accused of sexual assault, thrown into prison, and forgotten by those who had promised to help get him out. Though life remained bleak for Joseph at times, he knew God had an end goal that was greater than he could have dreamed (even though he did dream of it in a certain sense).

Many people try to say God is punishing those who are going through sustained hardship. I think this is false. Look at the story of the man born blind in John 9. An entire chapter is devoted to it, because Jesus was confronting a fundamental issue in Jewish culture.

The Jews were about to stone Jesus, because He had just claimed to be God (John 8:58), and as He was leaving the temple, He saw a man who had been born blind. His disciples asked Him, "Rabbi, who sinned, this man or his parents, that he was born blind?"

Some Rabbinical teachings held that a child could sin in the womb before birth and be born with some sort of defect. It was also believed that the child could be punished, if it had been conceived outside of marriage.

Jesus answered His disciples, "It was not that this man sinned or his parents, but that the works of God might be displayed in him." Jesus was in effect saying, "He's not being punished for anything, but God is going to use this form of evil (the man's blindness) to bring Himself glory." Jesus then proceeded to heal the man of his blindness—on the Sabbath for good measure.

Just for fun, read through the rest of John 9 and John 10 to see the far-reaching effects of this healing. God was trying to break through the thickly reinforced cultural shell of Judaism that was in some ways hindering their belief that Jesus could in fact be the Messiah. What a creative way for God to weave the simple evil of blindness into a multi-faceted good. Also, see Luke 13:1-9 for more of Jesus on this topic of suffering not being a direct punishment from God because of a specific sin. Of course, there are oftentimes natural consequences that develop out of sins we commit.

For further study, here are many of the references in the New Testament related to suffering as part of the lives of followers of Jesus. Some are historical accounts of suffering (Acts contains far more than are listed here), while other references are teachings on how believers should respond to suffering when it comes. The entire book of James might be the best example of this. This is not an exhaustive catalog but a good starting point:

Matthew 11:12
Luke 9:23-27; 17:33; 18:7-8; 21:36; 22:28-31
Acts 5:41-42; 7:54- 8:4; 9:10-16, 13:47-52
Romans 8:16-37
1 Corinthians 5:11-16; 15:54-58
2 Corinthians 1:3-11; 4:7-18; 6:3-10; 7:5-6; 8:1-5; 11:23-28; 12:7-10
Galatians 3:3-5
Ephesians 3:11-13; 6:10-20

Philippians 1:12-14; 1:29- 2:10; 3:7-11; 4:10-15
Colossians 1:28- 2:5
1 Thessalonians 1:6-8; 2:14-16; 3:1-10
2 Thessalonians 3:1-5
2 Timothy 1:8-12; 2:3-17; 3:1, 10-14; 4:6-8; 4:16-18
Hebrews 10:32-39
James 1:2-4; 1:12-17; 5:7-11

In Paul's epistles, some of these references might make more sense when the letter is read as a whole, since that's how they were originally read/heard.

I hope this helps a little to see how much a part of life suffering was for the early church. Comfort should come from the fact that we are never alone in suffering.

Why I Was Never an Atheist

"There is no God." A negative universal epistemic claim. In order to prove this, one would have to possess all knowledge of everything, everywhere, at the same time. The inside of this oval represents all knowledge in the universe. Please fill in the amount of knowledge you possess.

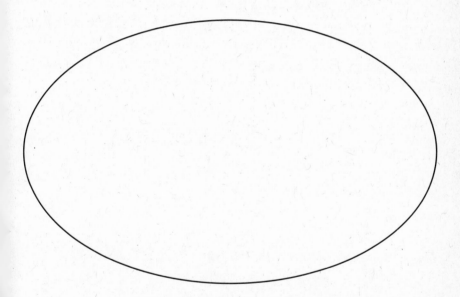

Based on the amount of knowledge you lack, can you prove or tell me with certainty that there is no God? No. It is logically impossible. Every atheist must have as much or more faith than any follower of Christ to believe the statement, "There is no God." Here's the irony. The only being who could possibly color the entire circle and *prove* atheism would be God Himself. Atheism is logically impossible to prove.

Appendix C

Grab Your Shovel

I was raised in church and believed in Jesus as my Savior at a young age. I believed the non-negotiable tenets of Christianity:

God is the creator/owner of everything . . . including me.
I am a sinner like everyone else.
No amount of good works could make me right with God.
Jesus is God's Son.
Jesus is fully God and fully man.
Jesus lived a perfect, sinless life.
Jesus died on the cross to pay for humanity's sin.
Jesus rose—showing God had accepted the payment.
Jesus' sacrifice canceled out my sin in God's eyes.
By believing in Jesus' sacrifice, I'll live eternally with God.

I also attended a Christian high school, which provided a plethora of unique and positive experiences. For instance, I received a solid biblical foundation (something I appreciate now more than I did at the time). On the whole, my teachers cared about me as a person, and I had healthy relationships with both teachers and other students.

There were also some cons.

Legalism.

Seemingly arbitrary rules abounded, and where this law grew, grace and love (in many cases) were choked out—something for which I've learned to take full responsibility. Gradually the love within my own faith began to wither as well, because I didn't know how best to deal with this conflict (and apparent contradiction) in preaching and practice. By the time I graduated high school, I was a hurting person. James said, "Faith without works is dead," (or better translated "unproductive"), and that described me.

I still believed all of the tenets mentioned above, but did I do anything with that truth? No. Did I pass the love God had shown to me on to anyone else? No. I knew God existed (He had shown up in my life far too often), but my love had been buried deep and replaced (almost unknowingly) with rock-solid bitterness. Bitterness toward what I saw as a closed-minded church rooted in tradition and an empty American dream—focused more on dress-codes, programs, building funds, and sound-systems than reaching out, sharing truth and showing Christ's love to the hurting outsiders and untouchables around the world—and in their own backyard. I know the Church should be outward focused—I just didn't see it.

I became disillusioned.

I thought, "I don't need a church or anybody else to help me along. I can develop my relationship with God all by myself. Besides, I understand me best." It took someone with major guts to reveal how selfishly myopic I had become.

During my freshman year of college, my eyes were opened to a young woman whose personality and outlook on life were as unique and beautiful as her name: Lael.

Lael was a growing believer; I thought I was too. After all, I could speak the lingo, and I played worship music at church every now and then. We had been dating for about a month, when she sat me down on the walk back from her dorm and asked, "So Jack, how would you say you've been growing in your faith lately? I mean have you been reading your Bible or sharing your faith with others . . . or anything?"

The question cut right through me. I froze like a deer in the headlights. For the first time, I stepped back and examined myself. With a deep sigh, I said, "I don't think I've really grown in my faith in years."

What followed was emotionally messy. Lael said I'd have to be the spiritual leader in our relationship, and since I clearly was not in any condition to fill that role, we would have to break up. She later told me it was hard to do, but that she knew it was the right decision. It wasn't a "holier than thou" thing. It was a "you need to work on that relationship, before we can work on this relationship" thing. Deep down—I knew she was right.

I went home and did some honest to goodness soul-searching. I talked with God. It had been awhile, and I was a little on the angry side. I figured I might as well be honest with Him, since He knew the truth anyway. I had deluded myself for long enough, so I told Him there was no desire inside of me to grow in my relationship with Him. I prayed the kind of prayer I have since prayed in a few other tough circumstances: "God, I don't have the desire for this, but I know it's right. Please give me a desire to grow in my relationship with You."

As usual, God gave me enough light for a baby-step. I realized I had let people cloud my view of Him. The church, including myself, is made up of millions of imperfect, sinful people who are bound to mess up and hurt each other. Count on it. Empirical. It wasn't fair for me to expect them to be perfect. God was saying, "If you're looking for that perfect church, you're not going to find it. So dig in where you are, help out, and get helped. Do this thing together: you, Me, them.

What had made me the judge of them? Shouldn't I have extended grace, like God had extended toward me? How could I expect to love the untouchables, when I couldn't even show love to my brothers and sisters who held my own beliefs?

Lael and I met up a week later to talk, and I was able to articulate and confess all of that nasty bitterness that had been festering for years inside my heart. With the bitterness cleaned out, I saw how good God truly is, and I began to look forward to reading the Bible.

I can point to that moment and say that my faith had truly become real in the sense of impacting how I lived my life. I am consistently learning to more readily give my plans and dreams up to God and trust that He will be completely faithful to lead me in the direction He sees fit . . . which right now is looking more and more like a remote tribe in Papua New Guinea.